French for Starters

Edith Baer & Celia Weber

Illustrations by Celia Weber

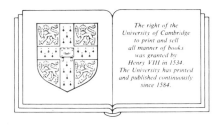

The right of the
University of Cambridge
to print and sell
all manner of books
was granted by
Henry VIII in 1534.
The University has printed
and published continuously
since 1584.

Cambridge University Press

Cambridge

London New York New Rochelle

Melbourne Sydney

Published by the Press Syndicate of the University of Cambridge
The Pitt Building, Trumpington Street, Cambridge CB2 1RP
32 East 57th Street, New York, NY 10022, USA
10 Stamford Road, Oakleigh, Melbourne 3166, Australia

First published 1986

Printed in Great Britain by Scotprint, Musselburgh

Library of Congress Cataloguing in Publication Data available

British Library Cataloguing in Publication Data
Baer, Edith R.
French for starters.
1. French language——Spoken French
I. Title   II. Weber, Celia
448.3′421   PC2121
ISBN 0 521 27043 X

What it's about

Whether you're a complete beginner, or just wanting to make a fresh start, 'French for Starters' puts you on the right track if you want to make yourself understood and understand what others say.

The first part of the book shows you how a minimum of language can take you a long way. The second part shows you how to use what you've learnt when you're shopping, socialising, travelling and so on. The cassettes provide vital backing to the book: they put you through your paces when it comes to speaking and getting the gist of conversations.

▶ Work systematically through the first ten chapters. Then tackle chapters 11–21 in any order you like: they deal with specific topics, some of which may interest you more than others. Always test yourself by doing the checkpoints. (The answers are given in the key in each chapter – a few are on cassette only.)

▶ There is a 'Language Summary' to refer to, a French–English/English–French Word List, and a list of Menu Terms.

▶ If you're learning with other people, look out for practice material in each chapter marked 'For groups'. Many of the checkpoints can be adapted for group use too.

▶ Always practise with the cassettes. They are full of examples, conversations and checkpoints (marked ⊡ in the book). Extra items, not printed in the chapters, are there to keep you on your toes. Use the pause button to give yourself time to imitate the speakers. To find your place easily jot down the counter number on your cassette recorder alongside the cassette symbol.

▶ To get the most out of the course give your French a short run every day rather than a weekly marathon. You'll get there faster in the end. **Bonne chance!**

CONTENTS

CONTENTS

It takes less effort to learn a few polite phrases in French than it does to plan your trip and pack your case.

1.1 'please' and 'thank you'

Try out these phrases, imitating what you hear on cassette. (If you haven't a cassette, see 'Sounding French' on page 5.)

s'il vous plaît (shortened to **svp** on notices)	please (also used to attract someone's attention)
oui, s'il vous plaît	yes please
merci	thank you
non merci	no thank you (**merci** on its own will also do to refuse an offer)
merci bien/merci beaucoup	thank you very much
de rien	you're welcome (in answer to thanks)
c'est très gentil	it's very kind of you

When you're talking to someone you don't know very well, including officials, it's polite to add

monsieur	to a man
mademoiselle	to a young woman or girl
madame	to an older or married woman

1.2 'hello' and 'goodbye'

Other people will probably say it to you first. Just echo what they say.

bonjour	hello, good morning, good afternoon
bonsoir	hello, good evening; goodnight (when you're leaving)
bonne nuit	goodnight (when it's bedtime)
salut!	hi! or 'bye! (very informal)
au revoir	goodbye
à demain	see you tomorrow
à tout à l'heure!	see you! (you may have heard people saying 'toodle-oo!': it's supposed to be the way the British soldiers said **à tout à l'heure** in World War I)

1.2 continued

Again, it's polite to add **monsieur**, **madame**, **mademoiselle**. Of course, if you know a person's name, use it!

Bonjour monsieur!   **Bonjour Monsieur Rousseau!**
Bonsoir madame!   **Bonsoir Madame Laforge!**
Au revoir mademoiselle!   **Au revoir Mademoiselle Martin!**

CHECKPOINT 1

Practise saying hello, good evening, goodbye, please, thank you to
1 the hotel manager   2 his wife   3 the young woman receptionist

▶ If you're talking to more than one person, **monsieur** becomes **messieurs**, **madame** becomes **mesdames**, and **mademoiselle** becomes **mesdemoiselles**. When you go into a shop, restaurant or café, you often hear **messieurs-dames**! It's short for **messieurs et mesdames**, and is just the conventional way of speaking to more than one person.

CHECKPOINT 2

What would you say in these circumstances? Practise saying it aloud.

CHECKPOINT 3

What do you say if

1 you want to attract someone's attention
2 you meet the manageress of the hotel in the morning
3 you want to refuse a glass of liqueur
4 you're saying goodbye to a young woman you're expecting to see again tomorrow
5 you're very grateful to someone
6 you're saying cheerio to someone you'll be seeing again later
7 you want to say a very informal hello
8 you want to acknowledge someone's thanks

1.3 Meeting people

enchanté (formal – spelt **enchantée** if you're a woman)	pleased to meet you
comment allez-vous?	how are you?
comment ça va?	how are things?
très bien, merci	fine, thanks
ça va!	fine!
et vous?	how about you?

It's normal to shake hands every time you meet or say goodbye, not just when you're introduced. Don't be surprised if people start kissing you on both cheeks when they've known you for only a while. It's not unusual to see two Frenchmen kissing each other in this way.

Imitate what you hear.

MONSIEUR ROUSSEAU   Ah, bonsoir Madame Laforge!
MADAME LAFORGE   Bonsoir, Monsieur Rousseau!
MONSIEUR ROUSSEAU   Comment allez-vous?
MADAME LAFORGE   Très bien, merci. Et vous?
MONSIEUR ROUSSEAU   Ça va, merci.

1.4 'excuse me' 'sorry' and 'OK'

pardon!   excuse me (if you want information, want to come past, reach for something), sorry (to apologise)
pardon?   sorry? (if you want something repeated)
d'accord!   OK!

CHECKPOINT 4

What do you say if

1 you've stepped on someone's foot
2 you're introduced to your host's young daughter
3 you meet a business acquaintance and want to know how he is
4 he asks how you are
5 he asks a question you don't hear properly
6 you agree to a suggestion

For groups

Practise saying to each other: hello, how are you, and the other phrases you've been learning.

1.5 **When things get difficult**

🔊 **je ne comprends pas**   I don't understand
pas si vite!   not so fast!
parlez-vous anglais?
vous parlez anglais?   do you speak English?

CHECKPOINT 5

1 There's a crisis! Stop a passerby and ask if he speaks English.
2 What do you say to a Frenchman who's talking too fast?
3 If you don't understand, what do you say?
4 If you want something repeated, what do you say?

CHECKPOINT 6

🔊 (a) Listen to the cassette and note down whether people accept (√) or refuse (×) what's being offered to them.

(b) Listen to the cassette and tick what people are saying.

1 good evening . . . goodbye . . . how are you? . . . you're welcome . . .
2 what did you say? . . . see you tomorrow . . . good morning . . .
3 I don't understand . . . how are you? . . . sorry? . . OK . .

CHECKPOINT 7

Practise making polite conversation.

1 You're sharing a table at breakfast with a French couple. Say good morning, first to the wife . . .
2 . . . then to the husband.
3 The wife says something you don't quite hear. What do you say?
4 She's talking too fast! How do you ask her not to?
5 The husband offers you a cigarette. Refuse politely.
6 Say goodbye to them both.
7 Later you meet a French colleague. How do you reply to his enquiry **Comment allez-vous?**
8 He introduces you to his wife. Shake hands and say . . .
9 She overestimates your ability to speak French. Tell her you don't understand.
10 But she just speaks more loudly. Find out if she speaks English.

KEY TO
CHECKPOINTS

1 1 Bonjour monsieur. Bonsoir monsieur. Au revoir monsieur. S'il vous plaît monsieur. Merci monsieur. 2 Bonjour madame. Bonsoir madame. Au revoir madame. S'il vous plaît madame. Merci madame. 3 Bonjour mademoiselle. Bonsoir mademoiselle. Au revoir mademoiselle. S'il vous plaît mademoiselle. Merci mademoiselle.

2 1 Merci monsieur. 2 Bonne nuit Pierre. 3 Au revoir madame. 4 Bonsoir mademoiselle. 5 Bonjour Monsieur Martin. 6 Au revoir messieurs.

3 1 S'il vous plaît! 2 Bonjour madame. 3 Merci (Non merci). 4 Au revoir mademoiselle, à demain! 5 Merci beaucoup (Merci bien). 6 A tout à l'heure! 7 Salut! 8 De rien!

4 1 Pardon! 2 Enchanté(e), mademoiselle. 3 Comment allez-vous? 4 Très bien, merci (Ça va). 5 Pardon? 6 D'accord!

5 1 Pardon monsieur, vous parlez anglais? (parlez-vous anglais?) 2 Pas si vite monsieur! 3 Je ne comprends pas. 4 Pardon?

6 (a) 1√ 2√ 3× (b) 1 Good evening. 2 See you tomorrow. 3 Sorry?

7 1 Bonjour madame. 2 Bonjour monsieur. 3 Pardon? 4 Pas si vite, s'il vous plaît madame! 5 Merci (Non merci). 6 Au revoir madame, au revoir monsieur. 7 Très bien, merci (Ça va). 8 Enchanté(e), madame. 9 Je ne comprends pas. 10 Vous parlez anglais? (Parlez-vous anglais?)

Sounding French

Now that you've tried out some phrases in French, concentrate on getting your accent right, but take it in easy stages. Always work with the cassette – it's much simpler that way!

▭ A very good idea is to mimic French people talking English with a very strong French accent. Imitate what you hear on cassette.

Now listen to them saying the same things in their own language and imitate them.

1.6 What makes it sound French?

There are some special features about the sound of French which you should try to imitate right from the start.

▶ Stress   The French tend to stress the last syllable of a word. Say these the French way:

▭ Pa<u>ris</u>   impor<u>tant</u>   ta<u>xi</u>   télé<u>phone</u>   prome<u>nade</u>   ca<u>fé</u>

▶ Nasal sounds Vowels followed by a single **m** or **n** usually have a 'nasal' quality about them. To make these sounds, talk *through* your nose – don't block it up! Imitate what you hear on cassette.

⌨ **am an em en** similar to *-ong* in *long*, but stop before the *g*
ambiance   restaurant   ensemble   encore

om on make the sound above with lips pushed forwards
comprends   pardon

im in ain ein similar to *-ang* in *bang* but stop before the *g*
impossible   vin   demain   frein

ien **en** after **i** rhymes with **vin** (see above)
bien   rien   canadien

um un similar to **im**, **in** etc
un   parfum

1.7 Guide to individual sounds

▶ Vowels There are often several different ways of writing the same sound as you can see from the list below. Sometimes they have an accent, e.g. acute (**é**), grave (**è**), circumflex (**ê**). This may affect the pronunciation. Accents are also used to distinguish between words with the same spelling, e.g. **la** (the) – **là** (there), **ou** (or) – **où** (where).

		nearest English sound	
⌨	**a à**	*u* in Southern English *must*	madame, voilà
	â	*a* in Southern English *mast*	âge
	ai aî	*e* in *get*	anglais, s'il vous plaît
	au	*o* in Northern English *rose* but shorter	autobus
		sometimes like *o* in *rot*	restaurant
	e	silent at the end of a word	madame
		er in *father*	je, le, demain
		before two consonants or **x**, like *e* in *get*	cigarette, excursion
		elsewhere like *ay* in N. Eng. *nay*	pied, parlez
	é	*ay* in N. Eng. *nay*	café, téléphone
	è ê ei	*e* in *get*	très, fête, treize
	eau	*o* in N. Eng. *rose* but shorter	beaucoup, château
	eu	*er* in *her*	fleur, jeune
		ir in *Birmingham* as pronounced by those who live there!	deux, peu, messieurs
	i î	*i* in *police* but shorter	vite, merci, dîner
	o	*o* in *rot*	cognac, occupé
		at the end of a word, like *o* in N. Eng. *rose* but shorter	zéro
	ô	*o* in N. Eng. *rose* but shorter	hôtel, côte
	oeu	*er* in *her*	coeur, oeuf
	oi	*wo* in *wonder*	bonsoir, Antoinette
	ou	*oo* in *moo*	vous, bonjour
	u û	*oo* in Scottish *good* ('guid') but longer	une, sûr
	ui	*wee* in *week* but shorter	nuit, suis

▶ Consonants   Most are similar to English, but these are different:

nearest English sound

 ç	*s* in *sound* (ꞔ is called a cedilla)	**français, garçon**
ch	*sh* in *shell*	**enchanté, château**
g	before **e** and **i** like *s* in *pleasure*	**gentil, Gigi**
gu	*g* in *garden*	**guillotine, guide**
gn	*n* in *news*	**cognac**
j	*s* in *pleasure*	**je, bonjour**
l ll	when it follows **i** sometimes like *y* in *way*	**travail, fille**
qu	always like *k* in *kick*	**qui, automatique**
r	like a brief gargle	**réservé, Pierre**
s	between vowels like *z* in *zoo*	**mademoiselle**
t	before **-ion** like *ss* in *pass*	**station**
th	*t* in *tea*	**thé**
w	*v* in *value*	**wagon-restaurant**
y	before a vowel like *y* in *yet*	**payez**
	elsewhere like *y* in *Yvonne*	**typique**

These are not pronounced:

h   (h)ôtel   (h)eure

d g p s t x z at the end of a word: **d'accor(d)   Edimbour(g)   beaucou(p)
e(t)   Bordeau(x)   parle(z)-vou(s)?** exceptions: **bus   terminus**

c in **blan(c)   estoma(c)   fran(c)   por(c)   taba(c); st** in **e(st)** (=is)

▶ Odd ones out   Where the pronunciation is unusual, it's generally explained in the text or on cassette, except for English words adopted by the French (called **franglais**) which may fox you on first hearing.

camping   parking   pub   sandwich   super   ticket   traveller

1.8 **Liaison**

Consonants which are usually silent (see above) are sometimes sounded when the next word begins with a vowel or **h**. This makes the words run together more smoothly, and is called liaison. French people aren't always consistent about making the liaison. From now on, it's usually indicated with a linking mark in the first part of the book.

▶ **s** and **x** are pronounced *z*; **les oranges   deux heures**

▶ **d** and **t** are both pronounced *t*, but the **t** of **et** (= and) is never sounded:

un grand hôtel   c'est ici   un café et un thé

▶ **n** of nasal sounds is usually linked to the next word: **un homme mon ami**

Read this aloud!

Try to get the sounds and the liaison right. Check with the cassette.

**Bonjour monsieur, comment allez-vous?
Pardon mademoiselle, vous avez mon ticket, s'il vous plaît?
Ma fille est arrivée à six heures
Voici mon adresse en Angleterre**

What you need to say

Sometimes it's possible to get what you want without saying anything.

Occasionally one word is enough (but no guarantee you'll be lucky!)

It's nearly always possible to ask for what you want with

a couple of words   or maybe three   or even four   adding **s'il vous plaît** for politeness

Une bicyclette,   un train électrique   et un paquet de cigarettes   s'il vous plaît!

2.1 **'a/an'**

Words for things as well as people are either 'masculine' or 'feminine' marked *m.* or *f.* in dictionaries.

The French for 'a' or 'an' is **un** with masc. nouns, **une** with fem. nouns.

un café	a café/a coffee	**une bière**	a beer
un hôtel	a hotel	**une chambre**	a (bed)room
un sandwich	a sandwich	**une cigarette**	a cigarette
un taxi	a taxi	**une glace**	an ice cream
un thé	a tea	**une pharmacie**	a chemist's
un timbre	a stamp	**une station-service**	a petrol station

CHECKPOINT 1

1 Stop a passerby and ask for the places you need if you want to find a room for the night, buy some cough mixture, fill up the tank.
2 How would you ask at the hotel for a room, a taxi, a coffee?
3 Call the waiter and order an ice cream, a beer and a sandwich.

2.2 **Numbers 1–10**

It's important to learn numbers. They crop up all the time in prices, exchange rates, distances, times, weights.

1 **un**	6 **six**	(**x** pronounced *ss* here)
2 **deux**	7 **sept**	(**p** is not sounded, but **t** is)
3 **trois**	8 **huit**	(**t** is sounded)
4 **quatre**	9 **neuf**	
5 **cinq**	10 **dix**	(**x** pronounced *ss* here)

CHECKPOINT 2

Practise counting from 1–10 again, imitating what you hear on the cassette. Then without looking at the text, count the sheep aloud. For extra practice, count them backwards, then count them in twos, starting with the even numbers. Then – if you're still awake – try the odd numbers!

un mouton   a sheep

For groups

Everyone in the group is given a number. If there are more than ten, divide into smaller groups. Anyone can start by calling out his/her own number and someone else's. That person repeats *his/her* own number and calls out another, and so on until a good fast rhythm is established, e.g. **six! deux! – deux! quatre! – quatre! neuf! – neuf! trois!** etc.

2.3 **Saying how many you want**

To ask for 'one' of something, use **un** with masc. nouns and **une** with fem. nouns in the same way as for 'a' (see 2.1).

un thé   one tea   **une glace**   one ice cream

In the plural, you usually add **s** to the noun, but don't pronounce it.

deux thés   two teas   **trois glaces**   three ice creams

You often don't sound the **q** of **cinq**, the **t** of **huit** or the **x** of **six** and **dix** when the next word begins with a consonant.

cinq timbres   five stamps   **huit sandwichs**   eight sandwiches
six paquets   six packets   **dix litres**   ten litres

If you're stuck for a word, say

un (deux etc) comme ça   one (two etc) like that

CHECKPOINT 3 — Who's asking for what? Fill in the correct letter next to each item. Then practise asking aloud for what everyone wants.

1 | Trois timbres > ...
2 | Quatre thés > ...
3 | Cinq paquets > ...
4 | Dix litres > ...
5 | Deux bières > ...
6 | Six comme ça! > ...

2.4 Saying how much you want

un kilo	one kilo (1 kg)	une bouteille	one bottle
une livre	one pound	une tasse	one cup
un litre	one litre	un verre	one glass

Link it to what you want with **de** (of) or **d'** before a vowel and often **h**.

un kilo		raisins	one kilo of grapes
deux bouteilles	**de**	vin	two bottles of wine
cinq paquets		cigarettes	five packets of cigarettes
un litre		huile	one litre of oil
une livre	**d'**	oranges	one pound of oranges
trois verres		eau	three glasses of water

CHECKPOINT 4 — How do you ask for

1 one glass of water   3 three packets of cigarettes
2 four cups of tea   4 two bottles of oil

CHECKPOINT 5 — Use the clues to complete the grid. The word in the shaded box should give you something useful to drink from.

You might ask for this

1 if you wanted to drown your sorrows
2 at breakfast time
3 if you insist on making your own orange juice
4 if you wanted to finish your picnic with some fruit
5 if you don't trust the tap water

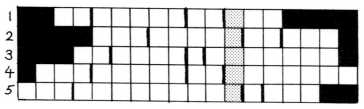

For groups — Take turns at ordering refreshments for your group.

2.5 **'the'**

There are four different ways of saying 'the'.

⊟ **le** with masc. nouns
le château   the castle
le patron   the manager, proprietor

la with fem. nouns
la carte   the menu
la gare   the railway station

l' with masc. and fem. nouns beginning with a vowel and often **h**
l'addition f.   the bill
l'hôtel m.   the hotel

les with all plural nouns (**les** rhymes with **clés**)
les clés   the keys
les toilettes the toilets

When you look up a new word, learn it together with **le**, **la** or **l'**.

CHECKPOINT 6

What do you ask for if you want to find

1 the market   3 the hospital   5 the airport
2 the post office 4 the telephones 6 the motorway

This is how they might appear in a dictionary:

aéroport m.   **hôpital** m.   **poste** f.
autoroute f. **marché** m.   **téléphone** m.

CHECKPOINT 7

You're meeting a friend for a meal at the station.

1 Ask at reception for a taxi
2 Tell the taxi driver your destination
3 Call the waiter
4 Ask for the menu – and later the bill
5 You're not satisfied, so ask for the manager
6 Before leaving, ask for the toilets

For groups

List the masc. and fem. nouns in this chapter, dictionary-fashion.
Test each other, asking 'What's the French for a . . . or the . . . ?'

2.6 **'have you a/the . . . ?'**	To check if they have what you want, start your request with **vous avez?** have you?, do you have? (i.e. you have?).

		une chambre?		a room?
Vous avez	**un verre?**	Have you	a glass?
	la clé?		the key?
	les sandwichs?		the sandwiches?

2.7 **'any'**	The word for 'any' will depend on what follows.

du with masc. nouns
Vous avez du vin?   Have you any wine?

de la with fem. nouns
Vous avez de la soupe?   Have you any soup?

de l' with all nouns beginning with a vowel and most with **h**
Vous avez de l'eau minérale?   Have you any mineral water?
Vous avez de l'huile?   Have you any oil?

des with all plural nouns (**des** rhymes with **clés**)
Vous avez des chambres?   Have you any rooms?

CHECKPOINT 8

How would you ask in a shop if they have any

1 grapes   3 cigarettes   5 lemonade (**limonade** f.)
2 oil   4 brandy (**cognac** m.)   6 perfume (**parfum** m.)

2.8 **'some'**	You also use **du, de la, de l', des** to mean 'some'. You can often leave out 'some' in English, but you can't do this in French.

du parfum   some perfume
de l'eau   some water
des verres   some glasses
du café, s'il vous plaît!   coffee please!
de la soupe, s'il vous plaît! soup, please!

Des aspirines, s'il vous plaît!

CHECKPOINT 9

Quick check. Fill in the gaps with **du, de la** etc.

1 . . . sandwichs 2 . . . thé 3 . . . vin 4 . . . bière 5 . . . tasses 6 . . . huile

For groups

Make a list of things for your partner to ask for in French (e.g. a packet of cigarettes, some wine, two oranges). Then reverse the roles.

Can you say it? **huit litres d'huile** (Practise with the cassette)

What you need to understand

Learning to speak French is only half the battle

Understanding it is the other half.

There are ways you can make it easier for yourself:

▶ Make an inspired guess (see 2.9)
▶ Try to pick up a few essential clues – forget about understanding every single word (see 2.10)

2.9 **Making a guess**

You can get clues from a number of things.

▶ The situation you're in

▶ A gesture or facial expression

▶ Words which are similar to English

un hôtel tranquille mais confortable   a quiet but comfortable hotel

2.10 **Homing in on key words and phrases**

The key words to listen out for (underlined on the next page) are often said emphatically, accompanied by shaking the head or by an apologetic gesture.

In many situations, people will answer in fairly predictable ways. For instance, if you ask for something or someone, you may hear **je ne sais pas** (I don't know) or you may be told either that they're available, or they're not.

2.10 continued   ▶ Not available

⌕ **je regrette/je suis désolé**   I'm sorry
c'est complet   it's full, fully booked
c'est fermé   it's closed
il n'y en a pas   there isn't any/there aren't any
Robert n'est pas là   Robert isn't in

CHECKPOINT 10   Fill in the missing key words. What's the message in each case?

key words: **pas   fermé   regrette   désolé   complet   là**

1 Bonjour monsieur, vous voulez visiter le château? Je . . . , c'est . . .
2 Bonjour messieurs-dames! Des chambres? Je suis . . . , l'hôtel est . . .
3 Oui mademoiselle? Des croissants? Il n'y en a . . .
4 Vous voulez parler au patron? Je . . . , Monsieur Guy n'est . . . . . .

▶ Available

Before you can get what you want, you may be asked to give more information, e.g. how much, how many? (**combien?**)

CHECKPOINT 11   What does the receptionist want to know?

TOURISTE   Vous avez une chambre, s'il vous plaît?
RÉCEPTIONNISTE   C'est pour combien de personnes?
TOURISTE   Pour deux personnes.
RÉCEPTIONNISTE   Et c'est pour combien de nuits?
TOURISTE   Pour trois nuits, s'il vous plaît.

CHECKPOINT 12   Cover up the text below and listen to the cassette until you get the gist of the conversation. Do they have what you want?

teabags **oui/non**   grapes **oui/non**   beer **oui/non**   mineral water **oui/non**

⌕   VOUS   Vous avez des sachets de thé?
VENDEUSE   Je regrette, il n'y en a pas.
VOUS   Et des raisins?
VENDEUSE   Je ne sais pas . . . Ah, oui! Vous en voulez combien?
VOUS   Un kilo, s'il vous plaît. Vous avez de la bière?
VENDEUSE   Oui, vous voulez combien de bouteilles?
VOUS   Quatre, s'il vous plaît.
VENDEUSE   Voilà! Et avec ça?
VOUS   Vous avez de l'eau minérale?
VENDEUSE   Il n'y en a pas pour l'instant.

For groups   Practise reading this conversation with a partner.

2.11 **Recognising numbers**   It's very important to recognise numbers when you hear them. So listen to 2.2 again on the cassette.

CHECKPOINT 13   Listen to the cassette. Fill in the missing numbers in figures.

       ⌨ ... kilomètres ... litres ... minutes ... timbres ... glace ... bouteilles

CHECKPOINT 14   ⌨ This one's more difficult. What's the misunderstanding?

Sidelines

When in France

▶ **taxi!**   You can rarely stop one in the street. Better to look for a taxi rank (**une station de taxis**) and wait at the front (**la tête de station**).

▶ **porteur!**   Few and far between. Better find a trolley (**un chariot**).

Not what they seem

un sandwich	part of a French stick cut lengthways, filled with cheese, ham, pâté or salami – often without butter
le patron	boss, proprietor or manager as well as patron – the feminine equivalent, or simply the manager's wife, is **la patronne**
raisins	grapes, not raisins

KEY TO
CHECKPOINTS

(**s'il vous plaît** is printed **svp**)

1   1 Pardon monsieur (madame, mademoiselle), un hôtel svp; . . . une pharmacie svp; . . . une station-service svp. 2 une chambre svp; un taxi svp; un café svp. 3 Garçon! Une glace, une bière et un sandwich svp.

3   1 b   2 d   3 e   4 a   5 c   6 f.

4   1 un verre d'eau; 2 quatre tasses de thé; 3 trois paquets de cigarettes; 4 deux bouteilles d'huile.

5   1 un litre de vin; 2 une tasse de thé; 3 un kilo d'oranges; 4 une livre de raisins; 5 une bouteille d'eau. The word in the shaded box is *verre*.

6   1 le marché; 2 la poste; 3 l'hôpital; 4 les téléphones; 5 l'aéroport; 6 l'autoroute.

7   1 Un taxi svp. 2 La gare svp. 3 Garçon! 4 La carte svp – l'addition svp. 5 Le patron svp. 6 Les toilettes svp.

8   1 Vous avez des raisins? 2 . . . de l'huile? 3 . . . des cigarettes? 4 . . . du cognac? 5 . . . de la limonade? 6 . . . du parfum?

9   1 des; 2 du; 3 du; 4 de la; 5 des; 6 de l'.

10   1 regrette, fermé (*castle closed*); 2 désolé, complet (*hotel full*); 3 pas (*no croissants*); 4 regrette, pas là (*Monsieur Guy isn't in*).

11   *For how many people? For how many nights?*

12   Non; oui; oui; non.

13   2   6   9   4   1   3

14   *He asks for* la station *instead of* la gare.

What you need to say

Getting exactly what you want may involve giving a few details.

Une jolie petite blonde,
s'il vous plaît,
divorcée, intelligente,
riche, charmante,
jeune, adorable...

AGENCE MATRIMONIALE

3.1 Describing things and people

Add a describing word (adjective). Some come before the noun, others come after.

▶ Before the noun

Some common adjectives, e.g. **bon** (good), **grand** (big, large), **petit** (small, little), **joli** (pretty), **jeune** (young), usually come before the noun.

un bon restaurant	a good restaurant
un grand paquet	a large packet
un petit magasin	a little shop
un joli appartement	a pretty flat
un jeune homme	a young man
une jeune femme	a young woman (**femme** rhymes with S. English 'rum')

CHECKPOINT 1

1 It has to be a small one: restaurant, shop, flat, hotel
2 Now make it a big one of everything: packet, glass, coffee
3 Each one has to be good: shop, wine, restaurant, perfume, film

▶ After the noun

Most other adjectives come after the noun.

un café noir		a black coffee
du vin rouge / blanc	some red / white	wine
un journal français		a French newspaper
du fromage anglais		some English cheese
un hôtel tranquille		a quiet hotel (**tranquille** rhymes with 'peel')

CHECKPOINT 2

What are or were they? Include **anglais** or **français** in your definition.

Cheddar   The Times   Beaujolais   Penny Black   Camembert

CHECKPOINT 3

You're looking forward to a restful evening. All you want is a good hotel, an English newspaper, a bottle of white wine and a large coffee. What will you ask for?

3.1 continued

▶ Masculine and feminine forms

Many adjectives change their form
when they describe a fem. noun.
But those which end in **-e** have
identical masc. and fem. forms.

un hôtel confortable	a comfortable hotel
une chambre confortable	a comfortable room
du vin rouge	some red wine
une rose rouge	a red rose

Most other adjectives add **e** (not pronounced) to the masc. form (the one given in the dictionaries) when describing a fem. noun.

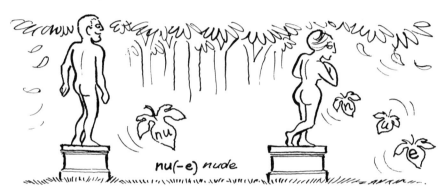

nu(-e) nude

You use the masc. form to describe masc. nouns.

un joli appartement	a pretty flat
un parking privé	a private car park
du fromage anglais	English cheese

You use the fem. form to describe fem. nouns.

une jolie femme	a pretty woman
une plage privée	a private beach
une voiture anglaise	an English car

Adding **e** to an adjective often means you sound the consonant before it. Practise making the difference between

un grand café – une grande plage
un petit restaurant – une petite femme
un parfum français – une voiture française

CHECKPOINT 4

Give the French for these and practise saying them aloud:

1 a French stamp, a French cigarette
2 a small hotel, a small bottle
3 a bottle of red wine, a red car
4 a large flat, a large room

CHECKPOINT 5   What would these people be likely to want?

1 English tourist wishing to keep up with the news
2 family wanting to eat out to celebrate an occasion
3 exhausted traveller in search of peace and quiet
4 wine-soaked reveller wanting to sober up
5 sun-worshipping naturists

CHECKPOINT 6   Complete the sailor-boy's prayer.

Sainte Marie, s'il vous plaît,   *une jo--- femme à Marseille,*   *une je--- femme à St. Malo,*   *une p----- blonde à Toulon*   *et un voyage calme!*

3.1 continued   ▶ Plurals

When you describe plural nouns, the adjective has to be plural too. You usually add **s** to the masc. or fem. form, but don't pronounce it.

deux grands cafés noirs   **six petites bouteilles**

If the adjective ends in **s** already, like **français** and **anglais**, don't add another one in the masc. plural.

un touriste anglais   **des touristes anglais**

CHECKPOINT 7   Describe what you want, choosing from these adjectives:

anglais   grand   noir   rouge   tranquille

1 trois cafés . . .   2 des roses . . .   3 des plages . . .
4 des cigarettes . . .   5 deux . . . chambres

CHECKPOINT 8   Sweet dreams!

a small castle
a young man
a big car
French wines
a pretty woman
a small private beach

Now dream in French!

For groups   Wishful thinking! Using the adjectives in this chapter, everyone can wish for three things. Something you'd like for a birthday? For Christmas? Right now?

3.2 'with' or 'without'

Put **avec** (with) or **sans** (without) in front of what you do or don't want.

une chambre avec douche   a room with shower
un hôtel avec piscine   a hotel with a swimming pool
une voiture sans chauffeur   a self-drive car

CHECKPOINT 9

These are your requirements. Describe them.

1 car   small, English, self-drive
2 flat   quiet, with private car park
3 hotel   big, with swimming pool, restaurant, private beach
4 room small, comfortable, without shower

3.3 Numbers 11–39

Make sure you can count easily up to ten (see 2.2). Then continue with

11 **onze**	16 **seize**	
12 **douze**	17 **dix-sept**	
13 **treize**	18 **dix-huit**	(pronounce **x** like **z**)
14 **quatorze**	19 **dix-neuf**	
15 **quinze**	20 **vingt**	(pronounce like **vin**)

After 20, pronounce the **t** of **vingt** and carry on like this:

21 **vingt et un**	26 **vingt-six**
22 **vingt-deux**	27 **vingt-sept**
23 **vingt-trois**	28 **vingt-huit**
24 **vingt-quatre**	29 **vingt-neuf**
25 **vingt-cinq**	30 **trente**

Continue in the same way up to 39. Check with the page numbers.

CHECKPOINT 10

Say these numbers in French. Check with page numbers as you go.

13 3 30; 2 10 22; 14 4 24; 1 11 21; 20 30 35;

25 5 15; 26 6 16; 8 28 18; 19 9 29; 27 17 7

3.3 continued

Tip! Put the numbers 1–39 (in figures) on cards. Write the French word for each number on the back. Spread them at random on the table, figures uppermost. See how many you can get right in 30 seconds. Keep these self-checking cards in an envelope and test yourself when you have a moment.

For groups

Play 'Buzz' in French. Start counting round the group **un, deux** etc. Any number with 3 in it, or which is divisible by 3, is taboo, and is replaced by the word **flûte!** (blast!). Drop out if you make a mistake or say a taboo number.

3.4 **Stating the price**

Price tags are marked in **francs** (**F** or **fr**) and **centimes** (**c**).
There are 100 **centimes** to the **franc**.
Use **à** (at) to link the thing you want to the price you want to pay.

une pâtisserie à sept francs	a pastry at seven francs
un timbre à vingt centimes	a twenty-centime stamp
deux paquets à huit francs dix	two packets at eight francs ten

CHECKPOINT 11

(a) It's the cheaper of the two you want every time.

(b) Now ask for the dearer of the two.

What you need to understand

3.5 **Read all about it!**

Advertisements and brochures are frequently peppered with adjectives to attract your attention. Many of these are easy to guess. Many are unimportant. So before rushing to the word list or a dictionary, try to get the gist of what you read.

★★ 15 place de la Gare

HÔTEL LA COLOMBE

situation unique
piscine chauffée
garage privé
restaurant avec menus variés
magasins à proximité immédiate

● BAR AMÉRICAIN ● MUSIQUE ●
● ATTRACTIONS ● TOUS LES SOIRS ●

Hôtel la Résidence
place Gambetta
confort moderne
toutes les chambres avec douche ou salle de bains
plage privée à 500m.
beaux jardins
vue sensationnelle

appartements

Le Paradis
boulevard Leclerc

● plage à 2 minutes
● grand confort   ● chauffage central
● cuisine – salle de bains
● terrasse individuelle
● prix avantageux

*avec vue exceptionnelle
à 150m de la plage
dans un ensemble
résidentiel calme*

APPARTEMENTS
les MILLE et UNE NUITS
avenue Montaigne

*jardins • grand parking
tout confort • téléphone
restaurants typiques à
proximité • prix modérés*

CHECKPOINT 12   (a) You want to stay somewhere quiet, with a good view, parking facilities, near the beach, not too expensive. You're keen on eating out. Which hotel or flat meets all your requirements? Underline the words which give you the information you need.

(b) Attractions listed in the brochures may turn out to be different when you get there. Your holiday accommodation had an unrivalled view over the railway station, you were kept awake by noisy music at night and woken up early by local shopkeepers opening up. Give the name and address of the place your friends should avoid.

3.6 **Recognising numbers**   This can be more difficult than learning to say them, especially when they're wrapped up in conversation. The next three checkpoints give you vital listening practice on cassette.

CHECKPOINT 13   ▱ Write down in figures the numbers you hear.

CHECKPOINT 14   ▱ Listen to what the waiter says as he makes out your bill. Is he right? You had

1 cheese omelette	23F
1 mixed salad	15F
2 glasses of red wine	6F a glass
1 ice cream	6F
a small black coffee	4F

CHECKPOINT 15   Fill in the missing numbers in figures.

(a) Paris est <u>à</u> . . . kilomètres d'ici.
(b) . . .F. . ., s'il vous plaît monsieur.
(c) La petite bouteille coûte . . .F, la grande coûte . . .F. . .
(d) Vous <u>avez</u> une pharmacie . . . rue de la République.
(e) Le film commence dans . . . minutes.
(f) Vous <u>avez</u> . . . minutes pour visiter le château.

For groups   Play Bingo in French, using the numbers 1–39. Draw your own grids of about six numbers. When all your numbers are up, call **loto!** Take turns to be the caller.

Sidelines

Not what they seem

un magasin	a shop, not a magazine (that's **un magazine**) – **un grand magasin** is a department store
sensationnel	fantastic, terrific, not sensational
joli	pretty, not jolly

DOUBLE
CHECKPOINTS

(Look back over chapters 1–3)

1   What do you say

to thank someone for being kind, to attract someone's attention, to refuse what's offered to you.

2   How do you say

See you tomorrow! Good evening! I don't understand.

3   How do you ask for

1 some soup 2 a petrol station 3 water 4 some oil 5 a stamp
6 a packet of cigarettes 7 four glasses of lemonade 8 the key

4   List all the words in the first three chapters which look similar in French and English. Note the ones where the meaning is different. Make sure you can pronounce them the French way (see 1.6, 1.7).

5   What were the captions to these pictures? Write them down, then look back and check.

KEY TO CHECKPOINTS

1 1 un petit restaurant, un petit magasin, un petit appartement, un petit hôtel; 2 un grand paquet, un grand verre, un grand café; 3 un bon magasin, un bon vin, un bon restaurant, un bon parfum, un bon film.

2 un (du) fromage anglais, un journal anglais, un (du) vin français, un timbre anglais, un (du) fromage français.

3 un bon hôtel, un journal anglais, une bouteille de vin blanc et un grand café.

4 1 un timbre français, une cigarette française; 2 un petit hôtel, une petite bouteille; 3 une bouteille de vin rouge, une voiture rouge; 4 un grand appartement, une grande chambre.

5 1 un journal anglais; 2 un bon restaurant; 3 une chambre (un hôtel) tranquille; 4 un café noir; 5 une plage privée.

6 jolie, jeune, petite.

7 1 noirs; 2 rouges; 3 tranquilles; 4 anglaises; 5 grandes.

8 (*woman*) un petit château, un jeune homme, une grande voiture.
(*man*) des vins français, une jolie femme, une petite plage privée.

9 1 une petite voiture anglaise sans chauffeur; 2 un appartement tranquille avec parking privé; 3 un grand hôtel avec piscine, restaurant et plage privée; 4 une petite chambre confortable, sans douche.

11 (a) la bouteille à neuf francs trente, les raisins à onze francs le kilo, le paquet à quatre francs vingt-cinq, les roses à vingt-huit francs.
(b) la bouteille à treize francs, les raisins à quatorze francs le kilo, le paquet à sept francs vingt, les roses à trente-cinq francs.

12 (a) Les Mille et Une Nuits. (b) Hôtel la Colombe, 15 place de la Gare.

13 1, 11, 21; 24, 14, 4; 5, 15, 16; 10, 9, 29; 18, 12, 2; 13, 30, 31, 3, 38.

14 *No, you had one ice cream, not two.*

15 (a) 12 (b) 16F25 (c) 11F, 19F20 (d) 15 (e) 2 (f) 30.

KEY TO DOUBLE CHECKPOINTS

1 1 Merci, c'est très gentil. S'il vous plaît! Merci (Non merci).

2 A demain! Bonsoir! Je ne comprends pas.

3 1 de la soupe; 2 une station-service; 3 de l'eau; 4 de l'huile; 5 un timbre; 6 un paquet de cigarettes; 7 quatre verres de limonade; 8 la clé.

What you need to say

4.1 Simple questions

The easiest way to put a question is to make a statement and make it *sound* like a question by raising your intonation (and also your eyebrows!). You'll hear questions like this in everyday spoken French much more often than you'll see them in print.

C'est confortable?   Mmmm, c'est confortable!

Imitate what you hear on cassette. Concentrate on making the difference between statement and question.

statement	question
C'est fermé	**C'est fermé?**
It's closed	Is it closed?
Il y a un tarif spécial	**Il y a un tarif spécial?**
There's a special rate	Is there a special rate?
Vous fumez beaucoup!	**Vous fumez beaucoup?**
You smoke a lot!	Do you smoke a lot?

4.2 'is it . . . ?' 'is that . . . ?'

Start your question with **c'est . . . ?**

C'est cher?	Is it expensive? (**cher** rhymes with 'air')
C'est ouvert?	Is it open?
C'est intéressant?	Is it interesting?
C'est libre?	Is it free? (i.e. unoccupied)
C'est loin?	Is it far?
C'est par ici?	Is it this way?
C'est le train pour Paris?	Is that the train to Paris?

C'est la patronne?

You can put your question more fully like this:

C'est loin, la plage?	Is it far to the beach?
	(i.e. Is it far, the beach?)
C'est par ici, la gare?	Is this the way to the station?
C'est <u>t</u>intéressant, le musée?	Is the museum interesting?

CHECKPOINT 1   What are they asking? Choose from these questions:

**C'est libre? C'est par ici, la plage? C'est <u>t</u>intéressant? C'est fermé?
C'est loin, l'oasis? C'est Madame Dupré? C'est le train pour Marseille?
C'est cher? C'est <u>t</u>ouvert?**

You may find a few amusing alternatives not given in the answers!

4.3 'is there . . . ?' 'are there . . . ?'

Start your question with **il y a . . . ?** which means both 'is there . . . ?' and 'are there . . . ?'

🖂 **Il y a**	**un coiffeur?**		a hairdresser?
	une piscine?		a swimming pool?
	du vin?	Is there	any wine?
	de l'eau?		any water?
	des excursions?	Are there	any excursions?

CHECKPOINT 2   You're checking with the local tourist office that your hotel has all the things it claims to have in the brochure. Ask if there's

1 a restaurant	3 a private beach	5 a swimming pool
2 a bar	4 a car park	6 a hairdresser

4.3 continued

▶ To find out if what you want is available locally, add **par ici** meaning 'round here' at the end of your question.

Il y a un parking par ici?	Is there a car park round here?
Il y a une boîte aux lettres par ici?	Is there a letterbox round here?
Il y a des magasins par ici?	Are there any shops round here?

CHECKPOINT 3

Ask if these can be found locally:

1 a petrol station   3 a supermarket   5 a chemist's
2 any shops   4 a letterbox   6 any museums

CHECKPOINT 4

You want to visit the castle at Blois. Find out if

1 it's far   4 it's interesting
2 there's a train to Blois   5 it's expensive
3 there's an excursion   6 there's a special rate

For groups

Ask each other if certain places of your own choice can be found locally. Partner can reply **oui, bien sûr!** (yes, of course!) or **non, je regrette!** or **je ne sais pas.**

4.4 **'do you . . . ?'**

Start your question with **vous**, as with **vous parlez . . . ?**, **vous avez . . . ?**

When you look up a verb in the dictionary, it will end in **-er**, **-re**, **-ir** or **-oir**. This is called the infinitive.

4.4 continued

▶ With **-er** verbs you make the **vous** form by replacing **-er** with **-ez**, both pronounced like **é** in **café**.

🖭 **fermer** (to close)
  Vous fermez à midi? Do you close for lunch (i.e. at midday)?
  habiter (to live, live in)
  Vous <u>habitez Paris?</u> Do you live in Paris?

▶ With other verbs, the **vous** form again ends mostly in **-ez**, but the way of forming it varies. Some of these verbs are given on page 142.

🖭 **connaître** (to know)
  Vous connaissez un bon garage? Do you know a good garage?
  ouvrir (to open)
  Vous <u>ouvrez demain?</u> Do you open tomorrow?
  vouloir (to want, want to)
  Vous voulez danser? Would you like to dance? (i.e. Do you want to dance?)

CHECKPOINT 5

Try finding out a few things.

1 (in the street) Ask that man if he knows a good restaurant.
2 (chatting to people) Ask if they live round here, if they want to visit the castle, if they know the manager/manageress.
3 (at the museum) Ask the attendant if they close tomorrow.
4 (in the department store) Ask the assistant if she speaks English.
5 (in a shop) Ask if they have any English cheese.

4.5 **'how much?' 'where?' 'when?'**

Start with **c'est . . . ?** or **vous . . . ?** as before, and include a question word. The ones you need most often are **combien?** (how much?), **où?** (where?), **quand?** (when?), **à quelle heure?** (at what time?).

🖭 **C'est combien?** How much is it?
  Vous <u>habitez où?</u> Where do you live?
  Vous fermez quand? When do you close?
  Vous <u>ouvrez à quelle heure?</u> (At) what time do you open?

Put your question more fully by adding a noun at the end (4.2).

C'est <u>à</u> quelle heure, le petit déjeuner?   What time is breakfast?
C'est quand, le festival?   When is the festival?

CHECKPOINT 6   You've just been told about an exhibition (**exposition** f.) to be held locally.
How do you ask where and when it is, and if it's interesting?

CHECKPOINT 7   How would you ask

1 (at the railway station)   What time is the train to Dieppe?
2 (in the tourist office)   When is the festival?
3 (the hotel receptionist)   How much is breakfast?
4 (at the cinema)   What time is the film?
5 (in a shop)   What time do you open tomorrow?

4.6 **'what's that?'**   ☐ **Qu'est-ce que c'est?**   What's that?
Not as difficult to say as it looks! It sounds a bit like 'keska-say'.

To find out the word for something in French, ask:
Qu'est-ce que c'est en français?   What's that in French?

To find out the meaning of a word, e.g. **diabolo-menthe**, ask
Diabolo-menthe, qu'est-ce que c'est?   What's a *diabolo-menthe*?

For groups   Work in pairs. Look over the different ways of getting information. Each
pair think of as many questions as possible which you could ask a hotel
receptionist, a railway clerk, a new acquaintance, a guide, a waiter, St Peter
(just for fun!).
The pair with the longest list of correct possibilities wins.

4.7 **Numbers**   ☐ 40 **quarante**   50 **cinquante**
40–69   41 **quarante et un**   51 **cinquante et un etc**
                      42 **quarante-deux etc**   60 **soixante etc** (pronounce **x** like *ss*)

Practise counting from 40–69 aloud and back again. Check with the page
numbers. Add the numbers to your self-checking cards (3.3).

What you need to understand

4.8 Understanding times

If you ask for information about opening and closing times, bus and train times, you need to be quick at recognising numbers or you may miss something important.

When you ask **c'est quand?** you may hear **dans . . . minutes, heures** (hours), **jours** (days), **semaines** (weeks).

dans dix minutes   in ten minutes
dans une heure   in an hour's time
dans huit jours   in a week's time (i.e. in eight days)
dans trois semaines   in three weeks' time

CHECKPOINT 8

1 Does the bar close in two minutes, ten minutes or two hours?
2 Is the festival tomorrow, in a week's time or ten days' time?
3 Is the manager expected back in three weeks, three hours or twenty minutes?

▶ When you ask **c'est à quelle heure?**, the answer may be given more precisely in clock times. Listen out for **heures** again, this time meaning o'clock (never left out as 'o'clock' often is in English).

à une heure   at one o'clock
à deux heures   at two o'clock
à trois heures cinq   at five past three
à quatre heures quinze   at four fifteen

Half past the hour is **à . . . heures et demie**.
à cinq heures et demie   at half past five

The 24-hour clock is widely used to distinguish a.m. from p.m.

à dix-sept heures trente (à 17h30)   at 5.30 p.m.

People often say **à midi** (at noon) instead of **à douze heures**, and **à minuit** (at midnight) instead of **à vingt-quatre heures**.

CHECKPOINT 9

You want to go to Paris for the day. You enquire about early morning trains, and trains for returning in the evening. Make a note of the departure and arrival times.

🖭 morning: departures . . . .   evening: departures . . . .
           arrivals   . . . .   arrivals   . . . .

4.9 **Understanding prices**

In answer to **c'est combien?** be careful to distinguish between **deux** (2), **douze** (12), **dix** (10); **trois** (3), **treize** (13), **trente** (30); **quatre** (4), **quatorze** (14), **quarante** (40) etc.

CHECKPOINT 10 🖭 Listen to how much each item costs and fill in the price tags.

4.10 **Coping with long answers**

When people want to be helpful, they may pad out their answers, even though a simple **oui** or **non** would be enough. But the padding may be useful, so you need to spot the key words (underlined).

C'est loin?	<u>Non</u>, ce n'est pas loin. C'est à <u>douze kilomètres</u> d'ici.
Il y a un tarif spécial?	<u>Oui</u>, il y a une <u>réduction</u> de <u>quinze pour cent</u> pour les <u>groupes</u> de <u>vingt</u> personnes.
Vous <u>ouvrez</u> demain?	<u>Oui</u>, bien sûr! De <u>huit heures</u> à <u>midi</u>, puis de <u>deux heures et demie</u> à <u>sept heures.</u>

CHECKPOINT 11

Cover up the text below while you listen to the conversation in the tourist office, then complete (a)–(g).

🖭 TOURISTE C'est loin, le château?
   HÔTESSE Non, ce n'est pas loin. C'est <u>à</u> soixante kilomètres d'ici. Quarante minutes par le train.
  TOURISTE C'est <u>ouvert</u> demain?
   HÔTESSE Oui, bien sûr. C'est <u>ouvert</u> tous les jours de neuf heures et demie jusqu'à dix-sept heures quarante-cinq.
  TOURISTE Et c'est cher?
   HÔTESSE Pour visiter le château et le parc, c'est dix francs cinquante, et cinq francs le musée. Il y a un tarif spécial pour les <u>enfants</u>, et une réduction de vingt pour cent pour les groupes de trente personnes.

(a) The castle is . . . kilometres from here.
(b) The journey takes . . . minutes by train.
(c) The castle is open from . . . to . . . .
(d) Admission charge to the castle and grounds is . . . .

(e) Admission to the museum costs . . . .
(f) Cheap rate for children: yes/no.
(g) Reduction of . . .% for parties of . . . people.

For groups

Read the parts of the tourist and tourist office clerk in checkpoint 11, changing times and prices for the rest of the group to jot down.

Sidelines

A matter of time

▶ **heure** can mean hour, o'clock and time

Il y a un train dans une heure	There's a train in an hour
Il y a un train à une heure	There's a train at one o'clock
Vous avez l'heure?	What's the time? (i.e. Do you have the time?)

▶ **une semaine** means a week, but you'll often hear **huit jours** instead

KEY TO
CHECKPOINTS

1 1 C'est cher? 2 C'est intéressant? 3 C'est libre? 4 C'est loin, l'oasis? 5 C'est fermé? 6 C'est Madame Dupré?

2 1 Il y a un restaurant? 2 . . . un bar? 3 . . . une plage privée? 4 . . . un parking? 5 . . . une piscine? 6 . . . un coiffeur?

3 1 Il y a une station-service par ici? 2 . . . des magasins par ici? 3 . . . un supermarché par ici? 4 . . . une boîte aux lettres par ici? 5 . . . une pharmacie par ici? 6 . . . des musées par ici?

4 1 C'est loin? 2 Il y a un train pour Blois? 3 Il y a une excursion? 4 C'est intéressant? 5 C'est cher? 6 Il y a un tarif spécial?

5 1 Pardon monsieur, vous connaissez un bon restaurant? 2 Vous habitez par ici? Vous voulez visiter le château? Vous connaissez le patron/la patronne? 3 Vous fermez demain? 4 Vous parlez anglais? 5 Vous avez du fromage anglais?

6 C'est où, l'exposition? C'est quand? C'est intéressant?

7 1 C'est à quelle heure, le train pour Dieppe? 2 C'est quand, le festival? 3 C'est combien, le petit déjeuner? 4 C'est à quelle heure, le film? 5 Vous ouvrez à quelle heure demain?

8 1 *In ten minutes.* 2 *In a week's time.* 3 *In twenty minutes.*

9 *morning: dep* 7.45   8.28 10.00 *evening: dep* 19.35 21.38 23.10
           arr 8.55 10.05 11.15   *arr* 20.40 22.57 00.15

10 *French–English dictionary 37F50, small bottle of brandy 42F40, box of chocolates 65F, sunglasses* (lunettes de soleil) *52F, packet of French cigarettes 7F60.*

11 (a) 60   (b) 40   (c) 9.30a.m.–5.45p.m.   (d)10F50   (e)5F   (f) *yes* (g) 20%, 30.

What you need to say

5.1 'where is ...?' 'where are ...?'

Start your question with **où est ... ?** where is . . . ?, **où sont ... ?** where are?

Où est la sortie?

🔲 **Où est**	**le guide, s'il vous plaît?**	Where's	the guide, please?
	la sortie, s'il vous plaît?		the way out, please?
Où sont	**les toilettes?**	Where are	the toilets?
	Monsieur et Madame Fauré?		Mr and Mrs Fauré?

CHECKPOINT 1

Ask where these are:

1 keys 2 bar 3 letterbox 4 driver 5 department stores 6 waiter
7 showers

5.2 **Asking the way**

If you want to say 'how do I/we get to . . . ?' use the phrase **pour aller à** . . . meaning 'in order to go to'.

🔲 **Pardon madame, pour aller à Pau?**　Excuse me, how do we get to Pau?
S'il vous plaît monsieur, pour　How do I get to Nice, please?
aller à Nice?

Remember it's polite to start with **pardon madame/monsieur** . . . etc or with **s'il vous plaît**.

Pardon messieurs, pour aller à Waterloo?

5.2 continued

▶ If you want to say 'to the . . .' you put

 **à l'** before all masc. and fem. nouns beginning with a vowel and most beginning with **h**

Pour aller	à l'aéroport?	How do I get	to the airport?
	à l'église?		to the church?
	à l'hôtel de ville?		to the town hall?

à la before all other fem. nouns
Pour aller à la gare?   How do we get to the station?

au before all other masc. nouns
Pour aller au camping?   How do I get to the campsite?

aux before all plural nouns
Pour aller aux grottes?   How do we get to the caves?

CHECKPOINT 2

From riches to rags! Complete the questions with **à**, **à l'**, etc.

1 Pour aller . . . Monte Carlo?
2 Pour aller . . . Hôtel Ritz?
3 Pour aller . . . banque?
4 Pour aller . . . casino?
5 Pour aller . . . jardins publics?

CHECKPOINT 3

Work out where everyone wants to go, then say how they ask the way.

For groups	Each person is given a piece of paper with half a dozen names of towns and of places in town (in English). Take it in turns to ask each other the way to them in French.

5.3 **'which . . . is it?'** **'what . . . is it?'**

You put **quel** before all masc. nouns, **quelle** before all fem. ones. The pronunciation is the same.

C'est quel numéro?	Which number is it?
C'est quelle adresse?	What's the address? (i.e. What address is it?)
C'est quelle rue?	Which street is it?
C'est à quel étage?	Which floor is it on?

CHECKPOINT 4

You want to know which one it is every time.

1 church   2 shop   3 flat   4 hotel   5 room   6 garage

5.4 **Numbers 70–80**

For the seventies, you don't need to learn any new numbers, but you have to be good at mental arithmetic! First look back over numbers 11–20. (3.3) You link them to **soixante**. Practise these numbers and add them to your self-checking cards.

70 **soixante-dix**	76 **soixante-seize**
71 **soixante et onze**	77 **soixante-dix-sept**
72 **soixante-douze**	78 **soixante-dix-huit**
73 **soixante-treize**	79 **soixante-dix-neuf**
74 **soixante-quatorze**	80 **quatre-vingts**
75 **soixante-quinze**	(i.e. 4 × 20, four score)

CHECKPOINT 5

Try saying these pairs of numbers. Check also with the cassette.

63:73   75:65   61:71   72:62   64:74   76:66   69:79   24:80   78:68   77:67

For groups	Team game. Each team member writes a number between 50–80 on a card and holds it up for someone in the other team to say in French. Hesitation and inaccuracy score 0. One point for each correct answer.

What you need to understand

5.5 **Understanding directions**

When you want to find places, you may be unlucky and get the answer **je ne sais pas**, or **je ne suis pas d'ici** (I'm a stranger round here). Or you may be given directions which often sound complicated. So you need to concentrate on picking out key words.

5.5 continued

à gauche to/on the left
à droite to/on the right
tout droit straight on

Although **droite** and **droit** look similar they don't sound quite the same. The **t** of **droit** isn't pronounced.

When you hear **se trouve à droite/à gauche** etc, it means 'is' or 'is situated on the right/left'.

CHECKPOINT 6

This is how your guide might point out various landmarks on a city tour. Cover up the text while you listen to the cassette. Make notes in English where these places are to be found:

1 the cathedral	5 St Peter's church
2 the opera house	6 the market square
3 the department stores	7 the museum
4 the town hall	8 the castle

La cathédrale St Jean se trouve à droite. C'est une cathédrale magnifique de l'époque de Charlemagne. A gauche, vous avez l'opéra. Tout droit, il y a les grands magasins. Tout de suite à droite, vous avez l'hôtel de ville et l'église St Pierre. A droite également, vous avez la place du Marché. A gauche, c'est le musée d'Art Moderne, et là-bas à droite se trouve le château.

► When you're told which way to go, you'll probably hear

continuez	carry on	**montez**	go up	**tournez**	turn
descendez	go down	**prenez**	take	**traversez**	cross

Vous montez le boulevard Clémenceau	You go up boulevard Clémenceau
Descendez jusqu'à la place Berlioz	Go down as far as Berlioz Square
Vous prenez la rue à droite	Take the street on the right
Tournez à gauche	Turn left
Vous continuez tout droit	Carry straight on

Et vous continuez tout droit, tout droit, tout droit

Sometimes people tell you **il faut** . . . you have to . . .

Il faut tourner à droite	You have to turn right
Il faut prendre la route de Calais	You have to take the Calais road

Before people give you any directions, they may ask you whether you're on foot (**vous êtes à pied?**) or going by car (**vous êtes en voiture?**).

CHECKPOINT 7

You're at the spot marked ◉ and want to get to the post office.

Follow the directions on cassette and say which letter on the map represents the post office.

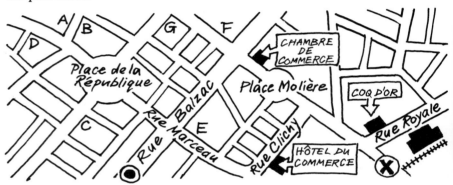

5.6 Locating the exact spot

To help you find the spot you want, people may relate it to another place or to the nearest landmark. Listen out for these key words:

en face de	opposite	**près de**	near
à côté de	next to	**au coin de**	on the corner of

C'est en face de l'hôtel de ville	It's opposite the town hall
C'est à côté de la pharmacie	It's next to the chemist's
C'est près du cinéma Vox	It's near the Vox cinema
C'est au coin de la rue	It's on the corner of the street

When you hear **c'est indiqué,** it means it's signposted.

CHECKPOINT 8

You're now at the spot marked ⊗ on the map above. You ask two passersby how to get to places. They don't agree.

Listen to the cassette, look at the map, and work out whether it's the man or the woman who directs you correctly to each of these places:

station. . . . Chamber of Commerce . . . good restaurant . . .

For groups

Listen to checkpoint 7 on cassette and act as interpreter for your partner, who can then do the same for you with checkpoint 8.

CHECKPOINT 9

Work out which letter on the map represents each of these places. Try not to look at the text while you listen to the cassette.

1 **l'Hôtel Métropole** . . .
2 **un parking** . . .
3 **la pharmacie** . . .
4 **l'université** . . .
5 **le marché** . . .

1 L'Hôtel Métropole? Vous descendez la rue Carnot et c'est à gauche, en face de l'église St Jean.
2 Vous avez un parking rue de la République. Vous descendez la rue Carnot. Vous tournez à droite, et c'est tout de suite sur votre droite, au coin de la rue Fauré.
3 La pharmacie se trouve à gauche, à côté de l'Hôtel Métropole.
4 L'université? Continuez tout droit, tout droit, tout droit! C'est à gauche près du pont Wilson.
5 Pour aller au marché, vous montez la rue Carnot. Puis vous tournez à gauche et le marché se trouve en face du Palais de Justice.

5.7 **Recognising numbers**

Look over the numbers 60–80 (4.7, 5.4). Make sure you can recognise the difference between the sixties and seventies.

CHECKPOINT 10

1 Write down in figures the numbers you hear on cassette.

(a) . . . .   (b) . . . .   (c) . . . .
(d) . . . .

2 Complete the addresses you're given on the cassette.

(a) . . . **rue de la République**   (c) . . . **place Verdun**
(b) . . . **avenue de la Libération**   (d) . . . **boulevard Victor Hugo**

For groups

Work with a partner. One of you looks at the 'key' and reads out the answers to checkpoint 5, the other writes down the numbers in figures. Make up some more of your own.

5.8 **Recognising 1st, 2nd, 3rd etc**

If people direct you to the 2nd street, 8th floor etc, the numbers you'll hear end in **-ième**.

deuxième second   **troisième** third   **quatrième** fourth

But 1st is **premier** before all masc. nouns, **première** before all fem. ones.

In writing they often appear like this:

1e   1er   1ière   2e   2ième   etc

5.8 continued

Vous traversez le premier pont	You cross the first bridge
Prenez la première rue à gauche	Take the first road left
C'est la deuxième porte à droite	It's the second door on the right
C'est au troisième étage	It's on the third floor

The word for floor is often left out.

Vous montez au premier	You go up to the first floor
Le bureau? C'est au sixième	The office? It's on the sixth floor

CHECKPOINT 11

You're in a department store, looking for various things. Note down which floor they're on. Cover up the text while you listen to the cassette.

perfumery . . . camping gear . . . records . . . restaurant . . . toilets . . .

Le restaurant? Il faut descendre jusqu'au soixante-dix-huitième!

VOUS	S'il vous plaît, où sont les articles de camping?
VENDEUSE	Les articles de camping sont au deuxième étage.
VOUS	Et c'est à quel étage, la parfumerie?
VENDEUSE	Pour la parfumerie, il faut descendre au premier.
VOUS	Et les disques?
VENDEUSE	Il faut monter au quatrième.
VOUS	Où sont les toilettes, s'il vous plaît?
VENDEUSE	Au deuxième, au quatrième et au cinquième.
VOUS	Et où est le restaurant?
VENDEUSE	Le restaurant est au cinquième étage. Vous prenez l'ascenseur jusqu'au cinquième, et c'est la première porte sur votre droite.

CHECKPOINT 12

Your hostess has sent you instructions on how to get to their flat. Summarise them (in English) for your friend who's driving. Underline the words that matter. Don't worry too much about the rest.

Chers amis

Voici comment trouver notre appartement. C'est très simple. Vous sortez du camping, vous tournez à gauche et vous prenez la 1ère route à droite. Puis c'est indiqué. Quand vous arrivez en ville, vous continuez tout droit jusqu'au centre. Vous descendez la rue Victor Hugo, puis vous montez la deuxième rue à gauche, la rue François Hibert. Nous habitons au n° 78 au quatrième. Il y a un petit parking au coin.

Au plaisir de vous voir!

Marie-Claire

Sidelines

Not what they seem

une place	square, not a place
une route	road, not a route
l'hôtel de ville	town hall, not the best hotel in town!

When in France

When you ask a policeman for information, address him as **monsieur**, or give him his full title, **monsieur l'agent**. Unless of course it's a policewoman . . .

KEY TO
CHECKPOINTS

1 1 Où sont les clés? 2 Où est le bar? 3 Où est la boîte aux lettres? 4 Où est le chauffeur? 5 Où sont les grands magasins? 6 Où est le garçon? 7 Où sont les douches?

2 1 à; 2 à l'; 3 à la; 4 au; 5 aux.

3 1 Pour aller à Chamonix? 2 Pour aller au marché? 3 Pour aller à l'Hôtel Le Paradis? 4 Pour aller à la plage? 5 Pour aller à l'aéroport? 6 Pour aller aux grottes?

4 1 C'est quelle église? 2 C'est quel magasin? 3 C'est quel appartement? 4 C'est quel hôtel? 5 C'est quelle chambre? 6 C'est quel garage?

5 soixante-trois, soixante-treize / soixante-quinze, soixante-cinq
soixante et un, soixante et onze / soixante-douze, soixante-deux
soixante-quatre, soixante-quatorze / soixante-seize, soixante-six
soixante-neuf, soixante-dix-neuf / vingt-quatre, quatre-vingts
soixante-dix-huit, soixante-huit / soixante-dix-sept, soixante-sept

6 1 *On the right.* 2 *On the left.* 3 *Straight on.* 4 *On the right.* 5 *On the right.* 6 *On the right.* 7 *On the left.* 8 *Over there on the right.*

7 B.

8 *the station – man, the Chamber of Commerce – woman, restaurant – woman.*

9 1 A   2 C   3 B   4 E   5 D.

10 1(a) 6 16 76   (b) 12 72 62   (c) 64 24 80   (d) 13 73 63.
2(a) 65   (b) 75   (c) 67   (d) 77.

11 *perfumery 1st floor, camping gear 2nd, records 4th, restaurant 5th, toilets 2nd, 4th and 5th.*

12 *Turn left after leaving campsite. First on the right, then it's signposted. Once you're in town, carry on to the centre. Go down* rue Victor Hugo, *take the 2nd left. They live at no. 78 on the 4th floor. There's a car park on the corner.*

What you need to say

6.1 'I am . . .'
'I'm not . . .'

Start with **je suis**, I am (from **être** to be), or more emphatically **moi, je suis.**

To describe your nationality, to say whether you're married or not – and other things about yourself – , add an adjective.

Je suis anglais

Et moi, je suis française

🙂 Je suis écossais		Scottish
Je suis gallois		Welsh
Je suis irlandais	I'm	Irish
Je suis marié		married
Je suis content		pleased

Remember to make the adjective fem. if you're a woman (3.1).

To say 'I'm not . . .' it's **je ne suis pas** (**marié, content** etc).

CHECKPOINT 1

Ladies only! Make all the examples feminine, and say them aloud.

▶ To say what your occupation is, start with **je suis** and add the noun for what you are, leaving out the word for 'a'.

🙂 Je suis	journaliste		journalist
	médecin	I'm a	doctor
	ménagère		housewife

Some words for occupations have a masc. and fem. form.

Je suis étudiant m. / **étudiante** f.	I'm a	student
Je suis coiffeur m. / **coiffeuse** f.		hairdresser

If you have no work, or are retired, say

Je suis au chômage	I'm	unemployed
Je suis retraité(e)		retired

▶ To say where you're from, add **de** (**d'** before a vowel) + name of town.

Je suis	**de Londres/Coventry**	I'm from	London/Coventry
	d'Aberdeen		Aberdeen

CHECKPOINT 2

(a) Give a description of yourself – your nationality, job, where you're from, what you're like, including some of these details for fun: **charmant, intelligent, joli, riche, jeune, modeste, élégant, timide, romantique, impossible.**

(b) People think you're married, Scottish, from Inverness, unemployed, free tomorrow. Deny it all!

▶ For these things you may want to say about yourself, start **je suis en . . .**

Je suis en	**voiture**	I'm going by car	
	vacances		holiday
	voyage d'affaires	I'm on	a business trip
	voyage de noces		honeymoon

Je suis en voyage d'affaires

Et moi, je suis en vacances!

For groups

Tell the rest of the group all about yourself. Try to learn the names for everyone's occupation.

6.2 'my'

There are three words for 'my'.

📺 **mon** before all masc. nouns

Je suis ici avec mon mari et mon fils (pronounced 'feece') — I'm here with my husband and my son

before fem. nouns beginning with a vowel and most nouns beginning with **h**

Vous connaissez mon amie? — Do you know my girlfriend?

ma before all other fem. nouns

Où sont ma femme et ma fille? — Where are my wife and daughter?

mes before all plural nouns (**mes** pronounced like **les** and **des**)

Je suis avec mes collègues — I'm with my colleagues
Et moi, je suis avec mes amis — And I'm with my friends

CHECKPOINT 3

Say you're with your wife/husband, friends, boss, daughter, sons.

CHECKPOINT 4

Describe yourself, starting with **je** each time, and assume that
(a) you're Irish, from Tipperary, a doctor, not married, on holiday with your boyfriend/girlfriend (**ami** m. / **amie** f.)
(b) you're a housewife, Welsh, from Abergavenny, on a business trip with your husband and your children

**6.3 'we are . . .'
'we aren't . . .'**

Start with **nous sommes** (we are) or **nous ne sommes pas** (we aren't) and add information as you did for **je suis** (6.1).

📺 **Nous sommes en voiture** — We're going by car
Nous ne sommes pas de Londres — We're not from London

An adjective after **nous sommes** has to be plural (3.1).

Nous sommes contents (masc. plural for all-male or mixed company)
Nous sommes contentes (fem. plural for women only)

CHECKPOINT 5   What could they say about themselves?

(pleased)   (English)   (not retired)   (French)   (not pleased)

▶ To say 'and I', it's **et moi**, followed by **nous**.

Mon mari et moi, nous sommes en   My husband and I are on our
voyage de noces!   honeymoon!

CHECKPOINT 6   You and your daughter are Scottish. You're from Stirling. You're not on a business trip, you're on holiday with friends. You're going by car. What can you say about yourselves?

CHECKPOINT 7   What is each person saying? Choose something suitable from the examples in this chapter. There may be more than one possibility.

For groups   Say what you all have in common as a group.

6.4 **'our'**   There are two words for 'our'.

📺 **notre** before all singular nouns
      C'est notre fils   This is our son
      Vou<u>s</u> avez notre adresse?   Do you have our address?

nos before all plural nouns

Nous somme<u>s</u> avec	**nos collègues**	We're with	our colleagues
	no<u>s</u> enfants		our children

CHECKPOINT 8   You're passing round holiday snaps of hotel, private swimming pool, car, children, French friends. Introduce each one with **notre** or **nos**, starting with **voici** (here is, here are).

6.5 Saying what you have/haven't got

Start with **j'ai** (I have), or **nous avons** (we have), from **avoir** (to have) (**j'ai** rhymes with **clés**).

🔲 **J'ai une grande maison**   I have a large house
J'ai quinze jours de vacances   I have a fortnight's holiday
Nous avons des problèmes   We have problems

To say you haven't a/any . . ., it's **je n'ai pas de . . .** or **nous n'avons pas de . . .** (**d'** before a vowel and often **h**). It's always **de** (**d'**), not **des**.

Je n'ai pas d'enfants   I haven't any children
Nous n'avons pas de voiture   We haven't a car
Nous n'avons pas d'argent   We haven't any money

J'ai des problèmes!

CHECKPOINT 9

You're a journalist, married, you and your other half have a house, garden, car and two dogs (**chien** m.). You haven't any problems!

(a) Tell your French friends all about yourself and what you have.
(b) Make it more interesting by piling on a few adjectives (see checkpoint 2). Remember to make them fem. or plural where necessary.

For groups

Keeping up with the Joneses! Work in pairs. X says what they have at home, e.g. **Nous avons une piscine**. Y replies **Nous n'avons pas de piscine, mais nous avons . . .** etc. X continues in the same way.

6.6 Numbers 80–1000

For the eighties you add **un**, **deux**, **trois** etc to 80. For the nineties you add **dix**, **onze**, **douze** etc also to 80 (see 5.4 and page numbers).

🔲 | | |
|---|---|
| 80 **quatre-vingts** | 90 **quatre-vingt-dix** (i.e. 4 × 20 + 10) |
| 81 **quatre-vingt-un** | 91 **quatre-vingt-onze** |
| 82 **quatre-vingt-deux** etc | 92 **quatre-vingt-douze** etc |

The hundreds are straightforward.

100 **cent**	200 **deux cents**
101 **cent un**	300 **trois cents**
102 **cent deux** etc	999 **neuf cent quatre-vingt-dix-neuf**

mille (pronounced 'meal') is a thousand, not a million.

CHECKPOINT 10

Say how much money you have. Check your answers with the cassette.

🔲 (a) 81F (b) 21F (c) 92F (d) 99F (e) 289F (f) 186F (g) 500F (h)1000F (i) skint!

6.7 Giving your age

Start **j'ai** (not **je suis**). Add your age, always followed by **ans** (years).

🔲 **J'ai vingt et un ans**   I'm twenty-one
Et moi, j'ai soixante-dix ans   And I'm seventy

CHECKPOINT 11   Put yourself in their shoes! Say how old you are.

For groups   (a) Continue the team game suggested in chapter 5 (after checkpoint 5),
                      including numbers up to 1000.
                      (b) Chat to a partner about yourself – name, age, personal possessions.

What you need to understand

6.8 **Personal**   Many start with **vous êtes?** are you? (from **être** to be), or **vous avez?** have
   questions   you? (from **avoir** to have), or with **quel est?** what/which is? But the main
                          clue is in what follows.

Vous êtes	**américain?**	Are you American?
	de quel pays?	What country are you from?
	en vacances?	Are you on holiday?

Vous avez des enfants?   Have you any children?
Quelle est votre adresse?   What's your address?

▶ *Name*   In formal situations you're likely to hear the word **nom** (name).
It sounds just like **non**!

Quel est votre nom?   What's your name?
Votre nom, s'il vous plaît!   Your name, please!

Otherwise the key word is **appelez** (from **s'appeler** to be called)

Comment vous appelez-vous? |
Vous vous appelez comment? | What's your name?

▶ *Occupation*   Questions about your job usually include **métier** (job),
profession (profession) or **travail** (work).

Quel est votre métier?   What's your job?
Qu'est-ce que vous faites comme travail?   What sort of work do you do?

Vous faites comes from **faire** (to do, to make), one of the few verbs where
the **vous** form does not end in **-ez**. The same goes for **vous êtes**.

▶ *Age*   The key word is **âge**. (For the answers you give, see 6.7)

Vous avez quel âge?   How old are you?

CHECKPOINT 12   🔲 Say in English what people want to know about you.

CHECKPOINT 13   Try filling in this form.

Nom .... Prénom .... Nom de jeune fille ....
Date de naissance .... Lieu de naissance ....
Nationalité .... Profession ....
Date d'entrée en France .... No. de passeport ....
Domicile habituel .... Adresse en France ....

CHECKPOINT 14   Complete the conversation below the picture by filling in what the girl
answered. Check with the cassette, then answer the questions.

JEUNE HOMME   JEUNE FILLE

🔲 Vous êtes en vacances?   . . . .
    Vous êtes de quel pays?   . . . .
    Qu'est-ce que vous faites comme travail?   . . . .
    Moi aussi, je suis étudiant! Je suis étudiant en
    médecine. C'est votre première visite en France? . . . .
    Vous êtes libre ce soir?   . . . .

    1 How long a holiday has she got?   3 What are their occupations?
    2 Why isn't she free tonight?   4 Has she been to France before?

For groups   Take turns at reading the parts of the young man and the girl. Make up
similar conversations of your own.

Sidelines   **Not always what they seem**

un médecin	doctor, not medicine
la médecine	medicine, i.e. what you study in order to be a doctor, not what you take to get well (that's **un médicament**)
une femme	wife as well as woman
une jeune fille	young girl, not young daughter – but **nom de jeune fille** means maiden name
anglais	often means British as well as English
les vacances	holidays, not vacancies

When in France

► The French have their own version of some of our place names.

Londres London   **Douvres** Dover   **Edimbourg** Edinburgh

► A fortnight may seem a little longer – the French say **quinze jours**, rarely **deux semaines**. Remember **huit jours**? (Sidelines, chapter 4)

DOUBLE CHECKPOINTS

(Look back over chapters 4–6)

1 How do you ask
1 Is there a swimming pool round here?   3 Is it far to the beach?
2 How do I get to the motorway?   4 Do you know a good hotel?

2 You've been a bit careless and can't lay hands on your passport, keys, car, French money, wife/husband! Ask where they are.

3 What are they saying? Fill in the gaps.

.... tarif.......? Nous ....   C'est......porte?

4 Spot the difference! What are they saying in each case?

5 (a) Cross off the numbers you hear:
15   21   60   12   19   40   89   5   16   81   50   6   2   99   4   10

(b) Fill in the prices in figures for these rooms:
with shower . . .   with balcony . . .   on the 3rd floor . . .   with breakfast . . .

6 Your local paper reports an interview with a visiting French actor.

> Twenty-nine year-old French actor François Duplessis is enjoying a week's holiday in our town. Still a bachelor, François has no plans for getting married in the near future, and said he can't afford to have a girlfriend at the moment! Pity! He has three cars, a large flat in Paris and a small country house in Cannes.

Listen to the actor's answers on cassette and spot the mistakes the reporter made.

Can you say it?   **J'ai quatre-vingt-un ans** (Practise with the cassette)

KEY TO CHECKPOINTS

1 Je suis écossaise . . . galloise . . . irlandaise . . . mariée . . . contente.

2 (b) Je ne suis pas marié(e), je ne suis pas écossais(e), je ne suis pas d'Inverness, je ne suis pas au chômage, je ne suis pas libre demain.

3 Je suis avec ma femme (mon mari), mes amis, mon patron, ma fille, mes fils.

4 (a) Je suis irlandais(e), je suis de Tipperary, je suis médecin, je ne suis pas marié(e), je suis en vacances avec mon amie (mon ami).
(b) Je suis ménagère, je suis galloise, je suis d'Abergavenny, je suis en voyage d'affaires avec mon mari et mes enfants.

5 Nous sommes contents. Nous sommes anglaises. Nous ne sommes pas retraités. Nous sommes françaises. Nous ne sommes pas contentes.

6 Ma fille et moi, nous sommes écossais(es). Nous sommes de Stirling. Nous ne sommes pas en voyage d'affaires, nous sommes en vacances avec des amis. Nous sommes en voiture.

7 1 Je suis journaliste. 2 Je suis de Coventry. 3 Je suis coiffeur. 4 Mon mari et moi, nous sommes en voyage de noces. 5 Je suis en voyage d'affaires/en vacances. (Mon mari et moi . . . !)

8 Voici notre hôtel. Voici notre piscine privée. Voici notre voiture. Voici nos enfants. Voici nos amis français.

9 (a) Je suis journaliste. Je suis marié(e). Ma femme (mon mari) et moi, nous avons une maison, un jardin, une voiture et deux chiens. Je n'ai pas (nous n'avons pas) de problèmes!

11 (a) J'ai soixante-cinq ans. (b) J'ai soixante-quinze ans. (c) J'ai quarante-huit ans. (d) J'ai onze ans. (e) J'ai quatre-vingts ans. (f) J'ai vingt-quatre ans.

12 *Are you married? Are you with your husband (wife)? Have you any children? Which country are you from? What's your job? What's your name? Do you live in London?*

14 1 *Two weeks.* 2 *She's meeting friends.* 3 *They're both students.* 4 *Once.*

KEY TO DOUBLE CHECKPOINTS

1 1 Il y a une piscine par ici? 2 Pour aller à l'autoroute? 3 C'est loin, la plage? 4 Vous connaissez un bon hôtel?

2 Où est mon passeport? Où sont mes clés? Où est ma voiture? Où est mon argent français? Où est ma femme (mon mari)?

3 Il y a un tarif spécial? Nous ne sommes pas d'ici. C'est quelle porte?

4 1 vingt bouteilles – une bouteille de vin; 2 à droite! – tout droit! 3 Il y a dix étages – C'est au dixième étage. 4 Vous habitez Paris? – Vous habitez par ici?

5 (a) 12   19   40   89   50   6   (b) 170F   195F   180F   175F

6 *No! He does have a girlfriend* (Bien sûr, j'ai une amie!). *He has a small flat* (un petit appartement) *in Paris and a large house* (une grande maison) *in Cannes.*

What you need to say

7.1 **Saying what you do, like etc**

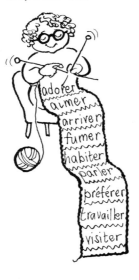

To say more about yourself you'll need to know more verbs. Remember that when you look one up it will end in **-er**, **-re**, **-ir**, **-oir** (4.4).

using verbs ending in '-er'

The largest and easiest group. They nearly all follow the same pattern, given in full in the Language Summary at the back.

parler   to speak

je parle	I speak/am speaking
nous parlons	we speak/are speaking
vous parlez	you speak/are speaking

▶ To make the form which goes with **je** (**j'** before a vowel and **h**) you normally replace the **-er** ending with **-e** (not pronounced).

J'arrive à neuf heures	I'm arriving at nine o'clock
J'habite Douvres	I live in Dover
Je travaille dans une banque	I work in a bank

To say you don't . . . , add **ne** (**n'**) . . . **pas**, as in **je ne comprends pas.**

Je ne parle pas espagnol	I don't speak Spanish
Je ne fume pas	I don't smoke

When you talk about likes and dislikes, always put **le**, **la**, **l'** or **les** before the noun.

J'aime la France	I like/love France
Je n'aime pas le vin	I don't like wine
J'adore les chats	I adore cats

C'est très gentil! J'adore les fleurs!

CHECKPOINT 1   Assume you're each of these people. What can you say about yourself?

		job	marital status	where you live	languages you speak	things you like √ or dislike ×
	1	doctor	married	Dover	English	children √ dogs ×
	2	guide	married	Edinburgh	Spanish	English beer √ cheese ×
	3	student	not married	London	French	French cigarettes × France √

For groups   Talk to a partner about yourself, using the headings in checkpoint 1 to guide your conversation.

7.1 continued   ▶ To make the form which goes with **nous**, replace the **-er** ending with **-ons**.

Nous habitons un petit village   We live in a small village
Nous n'aimons pas les grandes villes   We don't like big towns

Nous aimons Paris,   *mais nous préférons Londres!*

CHECKPOINT 2   Fill in the correct part of the verb:

1 (parler)   Nous ne . . . pas français!
2 (travailler)   Je . . . dans une agence
3 (habiter)   Nous n'. . . pas ici
4 (arriver)   J'. . . demain soir
5 (adorer)   J'. . . la musique pop
6 (préférer)   Ma femme et moi, nous . . . la cuisine française

CHECKPOINT 3   You and your other half are retired, you live in a small house, you have a big garden, you love flowers, you adore children, you speak French and like France. What can you say about yourselves?

7.2 Saying where you're going

One verb doesn't follow the pattern of other verbs in **-er**: **aller** to go.

je vais   I go/am going
nous allons   we go/are going
vous allez   you go/are going

As with **pour aller à** (5.2) you use **à** to say 'to' a town (**je vais à Nice**), **à l'**, **à la**, **au(x)** to say 'to the' (**nous allons au théâtre**).

CHECKPOINT 4   How do they say where they're going?

7.2 continued   ▶ To say 'to' a country or region ending in **-e** or **-ie** you use **en**. If it ends
                      in anything else, you say **au(x)**.

🔲 **Je vais en Bretagne**   I'm going to Brittany
   Nous n'allons pas en Italie   We're not going to Italy
   Vous allez au pays de Galles? Are you going to Wales?
   Non, je vais aux Etats-Unis   No, I'm going to the United States

CHECKPOINT 5   Holiday chat. Fill in the missing words.

1 Je vais . . . Canada   3 Vous allez . . . Espagne?
  Et moi, je vais . . . France   Non, nous allons . . . Portugal
2 Vous allez . . . Bretagne?   4 Nous allons . . . Etats-Unis
  Non, nous allons . . . Normandie   Et moi, je vais . . . Danemark

7.3 **Saying what**   Add the infinitive after **je vais, nous allons, vous allez.**
    you're going
    to do   **Je vais visiter les caves**   I'm going to visit the wine cellars
                      Je vais passer quinze jours ici I'm going to spend a fortnight here
                      Nous allons dîner à huit heures We're going to have dinner at eight

CHECKPOINT 6   Say where you're going and what you're going to do.

                      1 France   going to speak French
                      2 Paris   going to visit Notre Dame
                      3 Brittany   going to spend a fortnight in a small hotel
                      4 Hotel Royal going to have dinner with Max
                      5 Wales   going to speak Welsh

For groups   Tell each other where you're going at the weekend and what you're going to
                      do. It need not be strictly true!

7.4 Saying what you like, dislike, prefer doing

You also add an infinitive to **j'aime**, **je préfère**, **nous aimons** etc, as you do with **je vais** etc (7.3).

Nous aimons jouer au tennis   We like playing tennis
Je préfère regarder la télé   I prefer watching television
Je n'aime pas écouter la radio   I don't like listening to the radio

CHECKPOINT 7

This is you – describe yourself!

You don't like watching television, you don't like going to the cinema, you prefer going to the theatre, you like playing tennis.

7.5 Saying more about yourself

using verbs ending in '-re', '-ir', '-oir'

They don't all follow a regular pattern, but the **je** form usually ends in **-s**, sometimes **-ds** or **-x** (not pronounced) and the **nous** form always ends in **-ons** (see Language Summary at the back).

attendre	to wait, wait for	**j'attends**	**nous attendons**
comprendre	to understand	**je comprends**	**nous comprenons**
connaître	to know (a person or place)	**je connais**	**nous connaissons**
descendre	to go down, get off	**je descends**	**nous descendons**
faire	to do, make	**je fais**	**nous faisons**
prendre	to take; to catch (bus, train etc)	**je prends**	**nous prenons**
partir	to leave	**je pars**	**nous partons**
sortir	to come out, go out	**je sors**	**nous sortons**
venir	to come	**je viens**	**nous venons**
pouvoir	to be able (to)	**je peux**	**nous pouvons**
vouloir	to want (to)	**je veux**	**nous voulons**

Je sors dans dix minutes

Nous attendons le bus   We're waiting for the bus
Je prends le train de midi   I'm catching the 12 o'clock train
Nous partons demain soir   We're leaving tomorrow evening
Je ne fais pas la cuisine   I'm not doing the cooking
Nous voulons deux bières   We want two beers
Je veux changer des travellers   I want to change traveller's cheques
Je ne peux pas venir   I can't come

CHECKPOINT 8

You've been mistaken for someone else. Explain that you don't live in Oklahoma, you're not American, you don't work in a shop, you don't know Monsieur Lafitte, you're not leaving tomorrow, you don't want to go to Grasse, you're not waiting for the guide.

CHECKPOINT 9 You and your other half are planning to visit your friend Georges. Fill in your part of the telephone conversation. Check also with the cassette.

GEORGES Alors, vous venez chez nous demain! C'est fantastique! Qu'est-ce que vous faites? Vous prenez le train de 7 heures?

VOUS *(Say you can't catch the 7 o'clock train, you're catching the 8 o'clock train. You're arriving at 11.15)*

GEORGES Vous connaissez la ville?

VOUS *(say no, you don't know the town)*

GEORGES Ecoutez, vous sortez de la gare, vous prenez l'autobus, le 22 qui va directement chez nous. Vous comprenez?

VOUS *(say yes, you understand – ask if it's far)*

GEORGES Non, ce n'est pas loin. Quinze minutes au maximum. Vous descendez au terminus, et notre appartement est juste à côté.

VOUS *(confirm: 'We take the 22 and we get off at the terminus')*

GEORGES C'est ça! Bon voyage – et à demain!

7.6 **Saying what you want/want to do**

Instead of saying **je veux** (I want), it's more polite to start **je voudrais** (I'd like), both part of **vouloir**, though nobody seems to mind when you start **nous voulons** (we want). To say what you want to do, put the infinitive next.

Je voudrais du vin	I'd like some wine
Je voudrais louer un vélo	I'd like to hire a bike
Nous voulons une chambre tranquille	We want a quiet room
Nous voulons acheter des souvenirs	We want to buy some souvenirs

CHECKPOINT 10 How do they say what they would like to do?

1 Michel: visit the wine cellars
2 Yvonne and Monique: hire bicycles
3 Pierre and Robert: go to the beach
4 Louise: have dinner in a restaurant
5 Claude: play tennis
6 Jacques: hire a small car
7 Françoise: do the cooking
8 Alain: go to the opera

7.7 **Asking if you may/can**

Start **je peux, nous pouvons** and add the infinitive. (See also 7.9.)

Je peux parler à Madame Laurent? May/can I speak to Madame Laurent?
Nous pouvons prendre des photos? May/can we take photographs?

CHECKPOINT 11 How would you ask if you can 1 hire a car 2 visit the exhibition 3 wait here 4 watch television 5 come this evening

CHECKPOINT 12   Make a list of all the verbs you've come across so far, writing in the **je**, **nous** and **vous** forms. Check with the Language Summary.

For groups   See who can compile the longest list of sentences saying what you like doing, don't like doing, or want to do. Set a time limit.

What you need to understand

7.8 **Questions you may be asked**

The questions people ask may be put in different ways. The way you've learned so far is colloquial.

🖭 **Vous aimez le jazz?   Vous habitez où?   Vous partez quand?**

In print and in more formal conversation the word order is different.

Aimez-vous le jazz?   Où habitez-vous?   Quand partez-vous?

People often start with **est-ce que . . . ?** which has no equivalent in English. It simply indicates that a question follows, but there's no change in the word order.

Est-ce que vous aimez le jazz?

Est-ce que may also come after question words like **où**, **quand** etc (4.5).

Où est-ce que vous habitez?   Quand est-ce que vous partez?

A quelle heure est-ce que vous sortez ce soir?

CHECKPOINT 13   Assume you're a different person for a while.

Vous habitez Bordeaux et vous travaillez dans un hôtel. Vous ne pouvez pas sortir ce soir. Vous aimez danser. Vous n'aimez pas la musique classique, mais vous adorez le jazz. Vous partez demain à dix heures.

🖭 Now answer (in French) the questions you hear on cassette.

▶ Many questions start with **qu'est-ce que?** (what?)

Qu'est-ce que	**c'est?**	What's that?
	vous désirez?	What would you like? (in a shop)
	vous prenez?	What will you have (to drink)?
Qu'est-ce qu'il y a à faire?		What is there to do?

When you hear **comme** in a question beginning with **qu'est-ce que . . . ?** you're being asked 'what sort of . . . ?'

	aimez comme musique?
Qu'est-ce que vous	prenez comme apéritif?
	voulez comme dessert?

Qu'est-ce qu'il y a comme pâtisseries?

CHECKPOINT 14   (a) Say in English what people are asking you.

(b) Listen again, then try answering in French.

7.9 When people talk about themselves

When people talk about themselves, they often start with **on** (one, you, people, we – in a general sense). The form of the verb usually *sounds* the same and is sometimes *spelt* the same as the **je** form (**on préfère – je préfère**). The exception is **aller** (**on va – je vais**).

On habite un petit village   We live in a small village
On va au cinéma ce soir   We're going to the cinema this evening

In very colloquial speech, people often say **nous** as well as **on**.

Nous, on adore l'Angleterre   We adore England
Nous, on ne comprend pas votre langue   We don't understand your language

When statements with **on** are made into questions (with a rising intonation, 4.1), they're suggestions to which you're expected to reply.

On va au cinéma ce soir?   Shall we go to the cinema this evening?
On prend un taxi?   Shall we take a taxi?

▶ When you hear **on peut?** it usually means 'may I/we?' or 'can I/we?'

On peut laisser la voiture ici?   May I/we leave the car here?
On peut regarder?   Can I/we have a look round?

CHECKPOINT 15   Summarise for your English friend what your French friend is saying.

Sidelines

Not what they seem

travailler	to work, not to travel
les travellers	traveller's cheques, not travellers (they're **voyageurs**)
la cave	wine cellar, not a cave (that's **une grotte**)

When in France

le sport   The French frequently adopt our words for names of sports and games, and pronounce them **à la française** (French-style). They're usually masc. e.g. **le tennis, le football, le rugby, le bridge.**

le vélo   To go cycling (**faire du vélo**) is still a very popular pastime in France. You can hire bikes from many railway stations.

KEY TO
CHECKPOINTS

1 1 Je suis médecin, je suis marié, j'habite Douvres, je parle anglais, j'aime les enfants, je n'aime pas les chiens. 2 Je suis guide, je suis marié, j'habite Edimbourg, je parle espagnol, j'aime la bière anglaise, je n'aime pas le fromage. 3 Je suis étudiante, je ne suis pas mariée, j'habite Londres, je parle français, je n'aime pas les cigarettes françaises, j'aime la France.

2 1 parlons; 2 travaille; 3 habitons; 4 arrive; 5 adore; 6 préférons.

3 Mon mari (ma femme) et moi, nous sommes retraités, nous habitons une petite maison, nous avons un grand jardin, nous aimons les fleurs, nous adorons les enfants, nous parlons français et nous aimons la France.

4 1 Je vais à la gare. 2 Nous allons au marché. 3 Nous allons aux grands magasins. 4 Nous allons à la plage. 5 Je vais à l'aéroport. 6 Je vais à Boulogne.

5 1 au, en; 2 en, en; 3 en, au; 4 aux, au.

6 1 Je vais en France. Je vais parler français. 2 Je vais à Paris. Je vais visiter Notre Dame. 3 Je vais en Bretagne. Je vais passer quinze jours dans un petit hôtel. 4 Je vais à l'Hôtel Royal. Je vais dîner avec Max. 5 Je vais au pays de Galles. Je vais parler gallois.

7 Je n'aime pas regarder la télé, je n'aime pas aller au cinéma, je préfère aller au théâtre, j'aime jouer au tennis.

8 Je n'habite pas Oklahoma, je ne suis pas américain(e), je ne travaille pas dans un magasin, je ne connais pas Monsieur Lafitte, je ne pars pas demain, je ne veux pas aller à Grasse, je n'attends pas le guide.

9 VOUS: Nous ne pouvons pas prendre le train de sept heures. Nous prenons le train de huit heures. Nous arrivons à onze heures quinze.
. . . Non, nous ne connaissons pas la ville . . . Oui, je comprends. C'est loin? . . . Nous prenons le vingt-deux et nous descendons au terminus.

10 1 Je voudrais visiter les caves. 2 Nous voulons louer des vélos (bicyclettes). 3 Nous voulons aller à la plage. 4 Je voudrais dîner dans un restaurant. 5 Je voudrais jouer au tennis. 6 Je voudrais louer une petite voiture. 7 Je voudrais faire la cuisine. 8 Je voudrais aller à l'opéra.

11 1 Je peux (nous pouvons) louer une voiture? 2 . . . visiter l'exposition? 3 . . . attendre ici? 4 . . . regarder la télé? 5 . . . venir ce soir?

13 J'habite Bordeaux. Je travaille dans un hôtel. Non, je n'aime pas la musique classique. Oui, j'aime danser. Non, je ne peux pas sortir ce soir. Je pars demain à dix heures.

14 (a) *What will you have? Will you have an aperitif? What sort of aperitif will you have? Do you like sport? What sort of sports do you like? Which do you prefer – football or rugby? Do you have a big car? What sort of car do you have? Do you have a French car?*

15 *They're leaving in two days' time. Going to spend a week with friends, but they're free tomorrow evening. They know a nice little bar near here. Can they ring us to make arrangements to have a drink together?*

8 TALKING ABOUT A PERSON OR THING

What you need to say

Elle adore les gadgets

8.1 Saying what someone does, likes etc

using verbs ending in '-er'

When you talk about another person, you use the same form of the verb as with **je** (7.1).

Moi, je travaille dans un bureau	I work in an office
Ma soeur travaille dans une agence de voyages	My sister works in a travel agency
Moi, j'arrive ce soir	I'm arriving this evening
Mon collègue arrive demain	My colleague arrives tomorrow

Use **il** for 'he' and **elle** for 'she'.

Mon père parle trois langues	My father speaks three languages
Il adore le français	He adores French
Ma fille n'aime pas travailler	My daughter doesn't like working
Elle préfère sortir avec des amis	She prefers going out with friends

▶ You use the same part of the verb with **on** (7.9) as with **il** and **elle**.

Ici on parle français	French spoken here

CHECKPOINT 1

What can you say about Chantal and André, using these verbs:
adorer aimer fumer parler regarder travailler
You may think of more things than are given in the key.

Hello Mr. Brown!

8.2 'he/she is going'

Remember, **aller** is different from other verbs in **-er**.

je vais	I go/am going		**nous allons**	we go/are going	
il	**va**	he goes/is going	**vous allez**	you go/are going	
elle		she			

Ma soeur va à l'hypermarché — My sister is going to the hypermarket
Elle va acheter des souvenirs — She's going to buy some souvenirs
Mon mari va à la banque — My husband is going to the bank
Il va changer des travellers — He's going to change traveller's cheques

CHECKPOINT 2

Quick check. Fill in the correct part of **aller**.

ANNE   Qu'est-ce que vous . . . faire demain?
PAUL   Ma femme . . . à la plage, et moi, je . . . visiter le château.
ANNE   Et votre fils, qu'est-ce qu'il . . . faire?
PAUL   Il . . . au match de football.
ANNE   Et ce soir, qu'est-ce que vous . . . faire?
PAUL   Ce soir, ma femme et moi, nous . . . au casino.

8.3 Saying more about someone

using verbs ending in '-re', '-ir', '-oir'

The form you need sounds exactly like the **je** form, although the spelling is different (7.5).

attendre	j'attends	il attend	partir	je pars	il part
comprendre	je comprends	il comprend	sortir	je sors	il sort
connaître	je connais	il connaît	venir	je viens	il vient
descendre	je descends	il descend	pouvoir	je peux	il peut
faire	je fais	il fait	vouloir	je veux	il veut
prendre	je prends	il prend			

Ma soeur connaît bien l'Angleterre — My sister knows England well
Notre ami part dans vingt minutes — Our friend leaves in twenty minutes
Il attend le taxi — He's waiting for the taxi
Il prend l'avion — He's catching the plane
Mon père ne sort pas aujourd'hui — My father's not going out today
Il veut écrire des lettres — He wants to write some letters
Et Anne? Elle fait la cuisine — And Anne? She's doing the cooking
Paul ne peut pas venir ce soir — Paul can't come this evening
Il vient demain — He's coming tomorrow

CHECKPOINT 3

How would you tell someone that

1 your boss is going to Dijon, he's catching the 9 o'clock train, he wants to consult a colleague
2 Claudette is going to Dover tomorrow, she doesn't know England, she doesn't speak English
3 Jacques is going to the cinema this evening, he likes American films, he's going out with a girlfriend
4 your father is doing the cooking this evening, he's making omelettes

For groups

Find out what your partner is planning to do this evening/tomorrow. Tell the rest of the group.

8.4 **'he/she has, hasn't . . .'**

You say **il/elle a** (from **avoir** to have)

j'ai	I have	**nous avons**	we have
il/elle a	he/she has	**vous avez**	you have

Elle a des idées originales !

🔊 | **Ma femme a les passeports, mais elle n'a pas les billets** | My wife has the passports, but she hasn't got the tickets |
|---|---|
| **Mon frère a deux enfants** | My brother has two children |
| **Il a une fille et un garçon** | He has a girl and a boy |

To say 'hasn't a/any' (6.5), it's **n'a pas de** (**d'** before a vowel and often before **h**).

Ma soeur n'a pas de voiture	My sister hasn't a car
Elle n'a pas d'enfants	She hasn't any children

CHECKPOINT 4

You're comparing what you have to what your sister and brother have.

1 You have a dog – your sister hasn't a dog
2 You have a large house – she has a small flat
3 You have two daughters – she hasn't any children
4 You have a fortnight's holiday – your brother has a week's holiday
5 You have an English car – he has a French car
6 You have problems with your daughters – he has problems with the car

▶ Remember that you also use **avoir** to say how old someone is.

Mon frère a trente-six ans	My brother is thirty-six
Notre bébé a six mois	Our baby is six months old

CHECKPOINT 5

Write a few sentences about Robert and Martine.

Robert is 30. He has a charming wife. He has a big American car. He doesn't like working in an office.
Martine is 25. She has a small car. She wants to go to Italy, but she doesn't have any money.

For groups

Exchange similar information as in checkpoints 4 and 5 about yourself and a friend or relative.

8.5 Going into more details

You describe someone's nationality, profession etc in the same way as when you're talking about yourself (6.1) but you say **il est** (he is), **elle est** (she is).

☺ **Philippe est homme d'affaires**   Philippe is a businessman
Il est canadien   He's Canadian
Il est de Québec   He's from Quebec
Jacqueline est secrétaire   Jacqueline is a secretary
Elle n'est pas française   She isn't French
Elle est de Bruxelles   She's from Brussels

CHECKPOINT 6

Starting with **il** or **elle**, what can you say about

1 The man next door: businessman, not English, from Rome
2 The girl upstairs: Spanish, from Madrid, hairdresser, not married

▶ When talking about a woman, remember that you usually add **-e** to the adjective (3.1, 6.1). But with some adjectives, you make other changes.

	masc.	fem.	
Most adjectives ending in **-x** change to **-se**	**affreux** **jaloux**	**affreuse** **jalouse**	awful jealous
Those ending in **-en** and **-on** change to **-enne** and **-onne**	**canadien** **bon**	**canadienne** **bonne**	Canadian good
Those ending in **-el** and **-il** change to **-elle** and **-ille**	**sensationnel** **gentil**	**sensationnelle** **gentille**	terrific kind, nice
Two with special forms	**vieux (vieil)** **beau (bel)**	**vieille** **belle**	old beautiful, good-looking

Both **beau** and **vieux** come before the noun like **bon**, **grand** (3.1). Before masc. sing. nouns beginning with a vowel and often **h**, they change to **bel** and **vieil** (**vieil** and **vieille** are both pronounced 'vee-ay').

Hippolyte est adorable! Elle est belle, généreuse — et très intelligente

Hippocrate est un bel animal. Il est très élégant, généreux, romantique — et il n'est pas timide!

☺ **Monsieur Blanc est parisien**   Monsieur Blanc is Parisian
Il est très vieux et très gentil   He's very old and very nice
Georges est un vieil ami   George is an old friend
Madame Giraud est une belle femme   Madame Giraud is a beautiful woman
Elle est sensationnelle!   She's terrific!

CHECKPOINT 7   Say a few words about these people:

1 Michel is Canadian. He's very kind, but he's not very intelligent.
2 Claudette is an old friend. She's very nice. She's very generous.
3 Chantal is a very good friend. She's terrific!
4 Guy is an old friend. He's not good-looking, but he's charming.

For groups   Describe your husband/wife or friend to a partner, using some of the
                    adjectives in 8.5, 6.1 and 3.1. Then try giving a pen-portrait of the
                    man/woman of your dreams.

8.6 **'his' and 'her'**   There are three words for 'his' or 'her' – **son, sa, ses**. Which one you use
                    depends on what follows. Regardless of whether it belongs to a man or
                    woman, you say

son before all masc. nouns
    Claudine cherche son mari   Claudine is looking for her husband
    Voici son chapeau   Here's his/her hat

    before fem. nouns beginning with a vowel and often **h**
    Paul est ici avec son amie   Paul is here with his girlfriend
    Vous voulez son adresse?   Do you want his/her address?

sa before all other fem. nouns
    Vous connaissez sa femme?   Do you know his wife?
    Sa valise est ici   His/her case is here

ses before all plural nouns
    Anne sort avec ses amis   Anne is going out with her friends
    Marc cherche ses lunettes   Marc is looking for his/her glasses

CHECKPOINT 8   Quick check. How do you say

1		his car	6		his daughters
2		her flat	7		his flat
3	I like	his friends	8	I don't like	her friend Antoine
4		her daughters	9		her car
5		his friend Robert	10		her friends

Can you say it?   **Charles cherche son chapeau et ses chiens** (Practise with the cassette)

8.7 Talking about a thing

You use **il** and **elle** to refer to a thing as well as a person: **il** refers to a masc. noun, **elle** refers to a fem. one.

🔲 **Comment est la cuisine italienne?**   What's Italian cooking like?
Elle est très bonne   It's very good
Mon lit n'est pas confortable   My bed is not comfortable
– il est très dur   – it's very hard
Vous avez une douche?   Have you got a shower?
Oui, mais elle ne marche pas   Yes, but it doesn't work
Le film commence à quatre heures   The film starts at four o'clock
– il finit à six heures   – it finishes at six

CHECKPOINT 9

Referring to what's in brackets as **il** or **elle**, how would you say that

1 it starts today (**la conférence**)
2 it's arriving (**le train**)
3 it closes at six (**la pharmacie**)
4 it leaves at midday (**l'avion**)
5 it's not working (**l'ascenseur**)
6 it finishes at ten (**le concert**)

CHECKPOINT 10

Here's half the information you want. How do you ask for the rest?

1 **Le train arrive dans dix minutes** (ask when it leaves)
2 **La banque ouvre à neuf heures** (ask at what time it closes)
3 **Il y a un bon film au Roxy** (ask when it starts)
4 **Il faut prendre le bus** (ask if it goes to the station)

CHECKPOINT 11

You're being quizzed about your hotel. Start with **il** or **elle** each time.

1 **Comment est votre hôtel?** (very good)
2 **Et la patronne?** (awful)
3 **Et comment est la chambre?** (beautiful)
4 **Le lit est confortable?** (very hard)
5 **Vous avez une grande salle de bains?** (small)
6 **Comment est la cuisine?** (very good)

For groups

Everyone is given a card with a noun on it, e.g. **l'exposition**, **le concert**, **l'avion**, **l'ascenseur**, **la pharmacie**. Talk about what's on your card, starting with **il** or **elle**.

What you need to understand

8.8 Questions you may be asked

When you're being asked about your family, friends, home or belongings, the questions may be put like this (see also 7.8):

Il a quel âge, votre fils?	How old is your son?
Elle est comment, votre maison?	What's your house like?
Il s'appelle comment, votre frère?	What's your brother called?

or more formally, when the word order is different, like this:

Quel âge a-t-il, votre fils?
Comment est-elle, votre maison?
Comment s'appelle-t-il, votre frère?

The purpose of the **-t-** before **il** and **elle** is to make a smooth liaison.

▶ Questions about how someone is usually include **aller** as in **comment allez-vous?** (1.3).

Il va bien, votre père?	Is your father well?
Et votre femme, comment va-t-elle?	And how's your wife?

CHECKPOINT 12 You meet your sister's friends on holiday. Say in English what you're being asked.

CHECKPOINT 13 Try not to look at the text while you listen to this conversation. Then answer the questions.

MME OLIVIER	Vous connaissez Monsieur Alain?
MME LEBRUN	Oui, je le connais très bien. Il est très gentil.
MME OLIVIER	Qu'est-ce qu'il fait, Monsieur Alain?
MME LEBRUN	Il est directeur de banque. Mais il n'est pas là pour l'instant. Il est en Australie, en voyage d'affaires.
MME OLIVIER	Ah bon? Sa femme sort souvent avec un jeune homme.
MME LEBRUN	Un jeune homme? Il est comment?
MME OLIVIER	C'est un grand type blond avec une voiture italienne.
MME LEBRUN	Quel âge a-t-il, ce jeune homme?
MME OLIVIER	Oh, trente-cinq, trente-six ans. Il est sensationnel! J'en suis jalouse, moi! Moi aussi, je voudrais avoir un ami comme ça, beau, jeune . . .
MME LEBRUN	Un ami? . . . . . . *(Fill in the rest – it's on the cassette.)*

1 Where is Mme Alain's husband?	4 What is he like?
2 What is his job?	5 Does he have a car?
3 How old is the man often seen with Mme Alain?	6 Who is he?

Sidelines

Not always what they seem

un garçon	a boy as well as a waiter
gentil	nice, kind, not gentle
grand	tall, big or large, not grand

KEY TO
CHECKPOINTS

1 Chantal travaille dans un bureau. Elle parle anglais. Elle adore les fleurs. Elle aime le chien. André ne travaille pas. Il regarde le (un) journal. Il fume beaucoup. Il adore les femmes. Il aime le vin.

2 allez; va, vais; va; va; allez; allons.

3 1 Mon patron va à Dijon, il prend le train de neuf heures, il veut consulter un collègue. 2 Claudette va à Douvres demain, elle ne connaît pas l'Angleterre, elle ne parle pas anglais. 3 Jacques va au cinéma ce soir, il aime les films américains, il sort avec une amie. 4 Mon père fait la cuisine ce soir, il fait des omelettes.

4 1 J'ai un chien – ma soeur n'a pas de chien. 2 J'ai une grande maison – elle a un petit appartement. 3 J'ai deux filles – elle n'a pas d'enfants. 4 J'ai quinze jours de vacances – mon frère a huit jours (une semaine) de vacances. 5 J'ai une voiture anglaise – il a une voiture française. 6 J'ai des problèmes avec mes filles – il a des problèmes avec la voiture.

5 Robert a trente ans. Il a une femme charmante. Il a une grande voiture américaine. Il n'aime pas travailler dans un bureau. Martine a vingt-cinq ans. Elle a une petite voiture. Elle veut aller en Italie, mais elle n'a pas d'argent.

6 1 Il est homme d'affaires, il n'est pas anglais, il est de Rome. 2 Elle est espagnole, elle est de Madrid, elle est coiffeuse, elle n'est pas mariée.

7 1 Michel est canadien. Il est très gentil, mais il n'est pas très intelligent. 2 Claudette est une vieille amie. Elle est très gentille. Elle est très généreuse. 3 Chantal est une très bonne amie. Elle est sensationnelle! 4 Guy est un vieil ami. Il n'est pas beau, mais il est charmant.

8 1 J'aime sa voiture 2 . . . son appartement 3 . . . ses ami(e)s 4 . . . ses filles 5 . . . son ami Robert 6 Je n'aime pas ses filles 7 . . . son appartement 8 . . . son ami Antoine 9 . . . sa voiture 10 . . . ses ami(e)s.

9 1 Elle commence aujourd'hui. 2 Il arrive. 3 Elle ferme à six heures. 4 Il part à midi. 5 Il ne marche pas. 6 Il finit à dix heures.

10 1 Il part quand? 2 Elle ferme à quelle heure? 3 Il commence quand? 4 Il va à la gare?

11 1 Il est très bon. 2 Elle est affreuse. 3 Elle est belle. 4 Non, il est très dur. 5 Non, elle est petite. 6 Elle est très bonne.

12 *You're being asked how old your daughter is, if she likes playing with French children, what your son's name is, where your husband is and how your sister is.*

13 *The missing line is:* Mais ce n'est pas son ami! C'est son frère qui passe ses vacances ici!
1 in Australia, on a business trip; 2 bank manager; 3 35 or 36; 4 tall, fair; 5 yes; 6 Madame Alain's brother.

What you need to say

Ils ne parlent pas français, et Jules ne parle pas anglais!

9.1 Saying what people do, like etc

using verbs ending in '-er'

The verb form you need sounds the same as the form with **je/il/elle**, but it's written differently. It ends in **-ent** which you don't pronounce. If you do, people may not understand you.

Les hommes préfèrent les blondes!	Gentlemen prefer blondes!
Les Ecossais aiment le whisky	The Scots like whisky
Les Français parlent très vite!	The French speak very quickly!

When the company is mixed or all male, 'they' is **ils**.
When it's exclusively female, use **elles**.

Ils......   *Ils.......*   *Elles......*

Mes filles passent un mois en Espagne – elles adorent Madrid	My daughters are spending a month in Spain – they adore Madrid
Ma soeur et son fils n'aiment pas habiter Londres – ils cherchent une maison à Oxford	My sister and her son don't like living in London – they're looking for a house in Oxford

Notice that **à** means 'in' as well as 'to' a town (5.2)
        en means 'in' as well as 'to' a country or region ending in **-e** or **-ie** (7.2).

CHECKPOINT 1   Read these aloud and check with the cassette. Remember not to pronounce the ending **-ent**, but make the liaison (1.8) between **ils/elles** and a verb beginning with a vowel or **h**.

J'arrive à midi. Il arrive ce soir. Ils_arrivent demain.
Je dîne à huit heures. Il dîne ici. Ils dînent souvent à l'hôtel.
J'habite une maison. Il habite un_hôtel. Ils_habitent un_appartement.
J'aime aller à l'opéra. Elle aime aller au théâtre. Elles_aiment aller au cinéma.

CHECKPOINT 2   What can you say about these people?

1 They live in a flat
2 They work in Paris
3 They speak four languages
4 They smoke a lot
5 They love playing tennis
6 They're spending a week in Normandy

For groups   Read through checkpoint 1 again, taking a sentence each. Drop out if you pronounce **-ent** when it should be silent, or if you hesitate.

9.2 **Saying they are going**

Remember **aller** is different from other **-er** verbs (7.2, 8.2).

je vais   nous_allons   ils vont
il/elle va   vous_allez   elles vont

Mes_enfants vont_à la plage   My children are going to the beach
Ils vont faire du ski nautique   They're going to go water skiing

▶ You also use **aller** to say how people are (1.3, 8.8).

Anne et sa mère vont bien   Anne and her mother are well

CHECKPOINT 3   You're having a party. Say what everyone is going to do, starting with **il/elle, ils/elles**.
1 Jacques and Giles: going to buy some wine
2 Anne-Marie: going to buy some cheese
3 your brother and sister: going to the market
4 your daughters: going to do the cooking

9.3 **Saying more about people**

using verbs ending in '-re', '-ir', '-oir'

The form you need usually sounds different from the **je/il/elle** form. It doesn't follow a set pattern, but nearly always ends in **-ent** which you don't pronounce.

9.3 continued

Imitate what you hear on cassette.

🔊	attendre	il attend	ils attendent	partir	il part	ils partent
	comprendre	il comprend	ils comprennent	sortir	il sort	ils sortent
	connaître	il connaît	ils connaissent	venir	il vient	ils viennent
	descendre	il descend	ils descendent	pouvoir	il peut	ils peuvent
	prendre	il prend	ils prennent	vouloir	il veut	ils veulent

These verbs are given in full in the Language Summary on page 142.

Nos amis ne connaissent pas Paris   Our friends don't know Paris
Ils ne comprennent pas le français   They don't understand French
Ils veulent un guide en anglais   They want a guide book in English

CHECKPOINT 4

How would you tell someone that

1 your daughters are waiting for your sister, they're going to the concert, they're taking a taxi
2 your friends are leaving this evening, they want to catch the ten o'clock train, they're going to spend a week in Grenoble
3 Monsieur and Madame Pernod can't go out this evening, they're waiting for a friend
4 Carole and Yvonne are coming today, they know your father, they don't know your mother
5 your friends don't understand French, they want to buy a guide book in English

▶ Using **faire**, **avoir** and **être**

The form with **ils/elles** ends in **-ont** as it does with **aller**.

faire	il fait	ils font	être	il est	ils sont
avoir	il a	ils ont	aller	il va	ils vont

Distinguish between **ils sont** and **ils ont** by pronouncing the **s** of **ils ont** like *z*.

🔊	**Mes parents sont en Bretagne**	My parents are in Brittany
	Ils vont à Concarneau	They're going to Concarneau
	Ils ont quinze jours de vacances	They have a fortnight's holiday
	Aujourd'hui ils font une excursion	Today they're going on an excursion

CHECKPOINT 5

Fill in the gaps with the right part of the verb.

1 (être)   Mes frères . . . en Angleterre.
2 (aller)   Nos amis . . . à Marseille.
3 (faire)   Pauline et son amie . . . une excursion en Provence.
4 (avoir)   Elles . . . des amis à Nice.

9.3 continued

▶ To say 'they haven't a/any', it's **ils/elles n'ont pas de (d')**, as with **je n'ai pas de** (6.5) and **il/elle n'a pas de** (8.4).

Ils ont cinq chats, mais ils   They have five cats but they
n'ont pas de chiens   haven't any dogs

CHECKPOINT 6

Your poor friends! They're not going to France, they haven't a car, they're not going to buy a car, they haven't any money!
Tell your French friends about them, starting with **ils**.

For groups

Make a verb chain. The first student gives a verb in the infinitive (e.g. **aller**), the second one says the **je** form (e.g. **je vais**), the next one the **il** form and so on with **nous**, **vous** and **ils**. Speed and accuracy are important. Hesitant blunderers drop out!

9.4 **Describing people**

When you use an adjective after **sont**, you have to make it plural as you do after **nous sommes** (3.1 plurals, 6.3). These have special forms:

beau becomes **beaux** in the masc. plural
adjectives ending in **-x**, like those in **-s**, stay the same in the masc. plural

🖭 **Sita et son amie sont indiennes**   Sita and her friend are Indian
Elles ne sont pas libres ce soir   They're not free this evening
Ses amis sont jaloux   His/her friends are jealous
Ses fils sont très beaux   His/her sons are very good-looking

CHECKPOINT 7   The two old spinsters who live next door are very rich, charming, and have six cats and three dogs. The dogs are old and awful, but the little cats are beautiful. Complete this information about them.

Elles h. . . à côté. Elles sont très v. . . et très r . . . Elles sont c. . . Elles ne sont pas m. . . Elles ont six . . . et trois . . . Les c. . . sont v. . . et a. . ., mais les petits c. . . sont b. . .

9.5 'your'

	votre	before all singular nouns	
		Votre mari est français?	Is your husband French?
		Je n'ai pas votre adresse	I don't have your address
	vos	before all plural nouns	
		Vos chambres sont réservées	Your rooms are booked
		Où sont vos bagages?	Where's your luggage?

CHECKPOINT 8   **Votre** or **vos**? Fill in the right ones.

1 Où sont . . . fils?
2 Je ne connais pas . . . parents.
3 . . . valise est dans la voiture.
4 Vous avez . . . passeport et . . . billets?

9.6 'their'

	leur	before all singular nouns	
		Leur maison est très jolie	Their house is very pretty
		Où se trouve leur hôtel?	Where's their hotel?
	leurs	before all plural nouns	
		Ils attendent leurs amis	They're waiting for their friends
		Elles passent leurs vacances en Italie	They're spending their holidays in Italy

CHECKPOINT 9   Complete the sentences with **son, sa, ses, leur** or **leurs**.

① Ils aiment......voiture
② Il regarde.....passeport
③ Juliette parle à......mari
④ Romeo n'écoute pas.....femme
⑤ Romeo sort avec .....amies
⑥ Ils attendent......amies
⑦ Elle adore jouer avec.....enfants

CHECKPOINT 10   Fill in your part of the conversation with a woman you met on holiday.

VOUS	*(Ask if her sons speak English.)*
MME ALDO	Un peu, c'est tout! Ils parlent italien, mais c'est normal, leur père est italien.
VOUS	*(Tell her that your daughters are spending their holidays in Italy, but they don't speak Italian. Say they have Italian boyfriends. They're very nice.)*
MME ALDO	Elles sont où en Italie, vos filles?
VOUS	*(Say that they're going to spend four days in Rome and three days in Florence. They want to visit the museums, the beautiful churches and the old bridge.)*

9.7 **Talking about things**

You use **ils** and **elles** to refer to things as well as people (8.7, 9.1).

ils refers to masc. nouns or a mixture of masc. and fem. nouns,
elles refers to fem. nouns only.

La tour et le château sont ouverts?	Are the tower and castle open?
Non, ils sont fermés aujourd'hui	No, they're closed today
L'église et la chapelle sont belles – elles sont très vieilles	The church and chapel are beautiful – they're very old

CHECKPOINT 11   You've spent the day exploring the town. Comment on what you've seen, starting each sentence with **ils** or **elles**.

1 shops (close at midday)
2 perfumes (expensive)
3 ice creams (very good)
4 car parks (far from here)
5 lifts (don't work)
6 castle and museum (beautiful)
7 churches (very old)
8 toilets (awful)

For groups   Take turns at describing something in your town, starting with **il/elle**, or **ils/elles**. Others have to work out what you're describing.

What you need to understand

9.8 **Things to listen out for**

▶ When you hear people saying **ils** and **elles**, they aren't necessarily talking about people. They may be referring to things (9.7).

▶ Before a vowel and sometimes **h**, the **s** of **ils** and **elles** may puzzle you at first because it sounds like a word beginning with **z** e.g. **ils aiment, ils habitent**

▶ Check with 7.8, 8.8 the different ways you may be asked questions.

CHECKPOINT 12   Read this conversation, then answer the questions.

PHILIPPE	Vous connaissez François, mon frère, et Jeanine, sa femme?
MONIQUE	Oui, un peu. Ils ont un petit bébé, n'est-ce pas?
PHILIPPE	Oui, c'est ça. Ils viennent passer le weekend ici à Paris. Puis ils vont partir pour la Bretagne où ils ont une maison.

MONIQUE   Quand est-ce qu'ils arrivent?
PHILIPPE Aujourd'hui vers cinq heures. Ils sont en voiture. On va
          les inviter à dîner ce soir. Vous êtes libre, Monique?
          Voulez-vous dîner avec nous?
MONIQUE   Avec plaisir!

1 Who are François and Jeanine?   4 How long are they staying?
2 Have they any children?   5 Where are they going next?
3 When are they arriving?   6 How are they travelling?

CHECKPOINT 13   ⌨ You're given some information about a couple you're going to meet. Pass it on in English.

CHECKPOINT 14   ⌨ You're listening to people discussing the French, English and Italians, and making some sweeping generalisations. Work out who they're talking about by filling in the numbers (given on cassette) below the corresponding pictures. Give their nationality in French, e.g. **ils/elles sont . . .**

Sidelines

Not always what they seem

faire   not always 'to do' or 'to make' but sometimes 'to go', as in **faire une excursion** (to go on an excursion), **faire du ski nautique** (to go water skiing), **faire du camping** (to go camping)

When in France

français   with a small letter is the name of the language, or the adjective, e.g. **en français, du parfum français**. The same applies to **anglais** etc, e.g. **un journal anglais**.
Notice that you say **je ne parle pas français** (**italien** etc) but you have to say **je ne comprends pas le français** (**l'italien** etc).

les Français   with a capital letter means 'the French'. **Un Français** is a Frenchman, **une Française** a Frenchwoman. The same applies to other nationalities, e.g. **un Anglais**, an Englishman.

les Belges   The French make jokes about the Belgians in much the same way as the English make jokes about the Irish.

n'est-ce pas? means isn't it? don't you? wasn't it? don't you think? etc.
Don't confuse it with **n'est pas** (isn't).

KEY TO CHECKPOINTS

2 1 Ils habitent un appartement. 2 Elles travaillent à Paris. 3 Ils parlent quatre langues. 4 Ils fument beaucoup. 5 Ils aiment jouer au tennis. 6 Elles passent huit jours (une semaine) en Normandie.

3 1 Ils vont acheter du vin. 2 Elle va acheter du fromage. 3 Ils vont au marché. 4 Elles vont faire la cuisine.

4 1 Mes (nos) filles attendent ma soeur, elles vont au concert, elles prennent un taxi. 2 Mes (nos) ami(e)s partent ce soir, ils (elles) veulent prendre le train de dix heures, ils (elles) vont passer huit jours (une semaine) à Grenoble. 3 Monsieur et Madame Pernod ne peuvent pas sortir ce soir, ils attendent un(e) ami(e). 4 Cécile et Yvonne viennent aujourd'hui, elles connaissent mon père, elles ne connaissent pas ma mère. 5 Mes (nos) ami(e)s ne comprennent pas le français, ils (elles) veulent acheter un guide en anglais.

5 1 sont; 2 vont; 3 font; 4 ont.

6 Ils ne vont pas en France, ils n'ont pas de voiture, ils ne vont pas acheter une voiture, ils n'ont pas d'argent.

7 habitent, vieilles, riches, charmantes, mariées, chats, chiens, chiens, vieux, affreux, chats, beaux.

8 1 vos; 2 vos; 3 votre; 4 votre, vos.

9 1 leur; 2 son; 3 son; 4 sa; 5 ses; 6 leurs; 7 ses.

10 vous: Vos fils parlent anglais? . . . Mes (nos) filles passent leurs vacances en Italie, mais elles ne parlent pas italien. Elles ont des amis italiens. Ils sont très gentils . . . Elles vont passer quatre jours à Rome et trois jours à Florence. Elles veulent visiter les musées, les belles églises et le vieux pont.

11 1 Ils ferment à midi. 2 Ils sont chers. 3 Elles sont très bonnes. 4 Ils sont loin d'ici. 5 Ils ne marchent pas. 6 Ils sont beaux. 7 Elles sont très vieilles. 8 Elles sont affreuses.

12 1 *Philippe's brother and sister-in-law*; 2 *yes, a baby*; 3 *today, about five o'clock*; 4 *the weekend*; 5 *Brittany*; 6 *by car.*

13 *Monsieur and Madame Suchon are Belgian. They live in Brussels. Madame Suchon is of French origin and doesn't like Belgium very much. They often come to France. They rent a small flat and spend their holidays visiting friends. They're both very nice.*

14 (a) 5 ils sont anglais; (b) 2 elles sont italiennes; (c) 4 ils sont italiens; (d) 6 ils sont français; (e) 1 elles sont anglaises; (f) 3 elles sont françaises.

What you need to say

10.1 Saying what happened

using verbs ending in '-er'

To say what has happened, you use **j'ai, il a, nous avons** etc with the past participle of the verb you need, e.g. **oublié** (forgotten), **invité** (invited), **commencé** (started). To make the past participle (p.p.), replace the **-er** ending with **-é**. It sounds the same.

✉ **J'ai oublié mon passeport**   I have forgotten my passport
Nous avons invité vos amis   We have invited your friends
Le film a commencé   The film has started

When talking about the past in English, you often leave out 'have/has'. In French, you can't leave out **ai/a/avons** etc.

Le match a commencé à deux heures   The match started at two o'clock
Nous avons mangé chez Simone   We ate at Simone's place
Ils ont passé le weekend à Paris   They spent the weekend in Paris

Rex a mangé mon ballon de football

CHECKPOINT 1

Say what you've done today.

1 ate a sandwich at midday
2 changed some traveller's cheques
3 bought some souvenirs
4 you and your friends spent two hours in Bordeaux
5 you (i.e. all of you) visited the wine cellars

CHECKPOINT 2

Now say what your friends did, starting with **ils** every time.

watched television – listened to records – danced – played tennis

10.1 continued

using verbs in '-re', '-ir', '-oir'

The past participle is formed differently. There's no set pattern. Many end in **-u**, **-i**, **-is** or **-t** (don't pronounce the **s** or **t**).

	p.p.		p.p.
attendre (to wait for)	**attendu**	**prendre** (to take)	**pris**
perdre (to lose)	**perdu**	**comprendre** (to understand)	**compris**
recevoir (to receive)	**reçu**	**écrire** (to write)	**écrit**
voir (to see)	**vu**	**faire** (to do, make)	**fait**
finir (to finish)	**fini**	**ouvrir** (to open)	**ouvert**

J'ai écrit des cartes postales	I wrote some postcards
Vous avez fait les courses?	Have you done the shopping?
Ils ont vu un bon film	They saw/have seen a good film

► To say someone 'hasn't done/didn't do', start **je n'ai pas**, **il n'a pas** etc and add the past participle. Remember that after **ne (n') . . . pas**, 'a' or 'any' is **de (d')** (6.5, 8.4, 9.3).

Je n'ai pas reçu votre lettre	I haven't received your letter
Elle n'a pas fini son travail	She hasn't finished her work
Nous n'avons pas pris de photos	We didn't take any photos

CHECKPOINT 3

(a) Say what happened today, starting with **je** every time.
You caught the bus, did the shopping but didn't see Monique, visited the castle, took some photos, didn't write any letters, finished your work, didn't watch television.

(b) Your friend did the same things. Say what she did.

For groups

Get your partner to tell you some of the things he/she did or didn't do today, using some of these verbs: **acheter écrire faire fumer manger parler regarder visiter voir**. Then tell the others about it.

10.2 **Saying when**

Days of the week (all masc.)

lundi	Monday	**jeudi**	Thursday		
mardi	Tuesday	**vendredi**	Friday	**dimanche**	Sunday
mercredi	Wednesday	**samedi**	Saturday		

Both 'Monday' and 'on Monday' is **lundi**. The same applies to other days of the week.

🖵 **C'est quel jour aujourd'hui?**   What day is it today?
C'est lundi   It's Monday
Vous partez quand?   When are you leaving?
Nous partons vendredi   We're leaving on Friday

Other expressions of time

🖵 **hier**   yesterday   **ce matin**   this morning
le matin   in the morning   **cet après-midi**   this afternoon
l'après-midi in the afternoon   **cette année**   this year
le soir   in the evening   **l'année dernière** last year

Il a pris l'avion hier soir   He caught the plane yesterday evening
J'ai perdu ma clé ce matin   I lost my key this morning

Notice that 'this' is   **cette**   before fem. singular nouns
cet   before masc. singular nouns beginning with a vowel and mostly **h**
ce   before all other masc. singular nouns

10.3 Saying you went/have been

You use **je suis, il est** etc (not **j'ai, il a** etc) with **allé**, the past participle of **aller**. To say someone didn't go, start **je ne suis pas, il n'est pas** etc.

🖵 **Le matin je suis allé en ville**   In the morning I went into town
Mon fils est allé à la banque   My son went/has been to the bank
Il n'est pas allé à la plage   He didn't go to the beach

After **je suis, il est, nous sommes** etc, the past participle changes like an adjective (3.1, 6.1, 6.3). This doesn't affect the pronunciation.

Add **-e**   when it refers to a woman
Yvette est allée en Italie   Yvette went to Italy

Add **-es**   when it refers to women only
Ses filles sont allées à Nice   Her daughters went to Nice

Add **-s**   when it refers to men only or mixed company
Samedi soir, mon frère et moi   On Saturday evening, my brother
nous sommes allés au théâtre   and I went to the theatre

CHECKPOINT 4   Say where everyone did or didn't go, and when.

last year ✗	this year ✓	this morning ✓	Sunday ✗	Sun. afternoon ✓
ITALY	BRITTANY		Cathédrale	
Jacqueline	Yourself	You and your husband/wife	your parents	Paul
1	2	3	4	5

10.4 Saying you arrived, stayed, left etc

You also use **je suis**, **il est** etc with other verbs which express the idea of coming, going or staying. The ones you'll need to use most often are

arriver	**je suis arrivé(e)** etc	I (have) arrived etc
rester	**je suis resté(e)**	I (have) stayed
partir	**je suis parti(e)**	I left
sortir	**je suis sorti(e)**	I went out
venir	**je suis venu(e)**	I came/have come

Mon mari est sorti!

Again, you may have to add **-e**, **-es** or **-s** to the past participle (10.3).

Il est arrivé lundi	He arrived on Monday
Elle est partie hier	She left yesterday
Elles sont restées à la maison	They stayed at home
Ils ne sont pas venus ce matin	They didn't come this morning

CHECKPOINT 5

Say when everyone arrived and left, and say how long they stayed. (Make sure you put the right ending on the past participle.)

	arrived	*left*	*stayed*
Jacques	Monday	Wednesday	3 days
Marie-Claire	Tuesday	Sunday	6 days
Pierre & Charles	Thursday	Sunday	4 days
Annick & Colette	Tuesday	Saturday	5 days
you and your father	Thursday	Friday	2 days

CHECKPOINT 6

You've kept a diary of your holiday. Talk about what you did.

Friday	Arrived Paris 10 o'clock. Took taxi. Went to hotel.
Saturday	Went to Montmartre. Ate in a little café. In the afternoon caught train. Arrived Versailles half past three. Went to château. Visited gardens. Took photos.
Sunday	In the morning went to Jardin du Luxembourg. Wrote 10 postcards! Spent afternoon in Fontainebleau.
Monday	Jacques came at 4 o'clock. In the evening, we went to the cinema. Saw good film.

For groups

Tell your partner where you went for your holidays last year, and what you did. Then each person in turn tells the rest of the group if he/she went out or stayed at home last night.

What you need to understand

10.5 **Understanding what happened**

It's the past participles which give you the main clues about what has happened. Make sure you recognise those listed in 10.1 and 10.4.

CHECKPOINT 7

What information are you given about these people?

🔲 (a) Jean-Luc 1 didn't take your letter
                   2 didn't understand your letter
                   3 didn't get your letter

     (b) Hervé   1 stayed in the hotel   (c) Anne 1 has gone to a party
               2 went out   2 is somewhere around
               3 rested in the hotel   3 has left

10.6 **Understanding what it was like**

When people talk about the past, you often hear **c'était** meaning 'it was', 'that was'.

🔲 **C'était <u>un</u> weekend fantastique!**   It was a fantastic weekend!
Mais c'était cher!   But it was expensive!

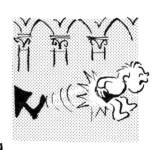

CHECKPOINT 8

Two people are talking about last year's holiday. Cover up the text while you listen to the cassette. Then answer questions 1–8.

🔲 CHANTAL   L'année dernière nous sommes <u>a</u>llés dans les Pyrénées. C'était formidable! Ce n'était pas cher, et nous <u>a</u>vons très bien mangé.

    CHARLES   Vous <u>a</u>vez fait du camping, n'est-ce pas?

    CHANTAL   Oui, mon mari adore ça. Nous sommes restés dans <u>un</u> très joli camping, et nous <u>a</u>vons fait des <u>e</u>xcursions à pied et en voiture. C'est <u>une</u> très belle région. Et vous, où êtes-vous <u>a</u>llés?

    CHARLES   Nous sommes <u>a</u>llés en Provence. Nous <u>a</u>vons passé quinze jours à Nîmes. C'était très <u>a</u>gréable, mais assez cher.

1 Where did Chantal go on holiday?
2 What was it like?
3 Where did she and her husband stay?
4 Was it expensive?
5 What did they do?
6 Where did Charles go?
7 How long did they stay?
8 What was it like?

Sidelines

When in France

Sunday is often a busy day. Most big football matches are played on Sundays, many food shops are open in the morning, and cafés and restaurants are crowded.

Not what they seem

rester	to stay, not to rest
faire les courses	to do the shopping, nothing to do with courses
à la maison	home, or at home, rarely 'to the house'
formidable	great, fantastic, not formidable

DOUBLE
CHECKPOINTS

(Look back over chapters 7–10)

1 Quick check. Fill in the gaps with **sont vont font** or **ont**.
To help you remember which verbs they come from, think of
je suis/ils sont, je vais/ils vont, je fais/ils font, but remember it's
j'ai/ils ont.

Jacques et Martine . . . français. Ils . . . charmants. Ils n'. . . pas
d'enfants. Ils . . . une belle maison près de Marseille. Ils . . . souvent au
centre ville. Ils . . . les courses, ils dînent en ville, puis ils . . . au théâtre
ou au cinéma.

2 Your children have made friends with some French children. You get
talking to their parents. Find out how old their children are, if they speak
English, if they play tennis, if they go water skiing, if they like going out
with their English friends.

3 It has been one of those days! You've forgotten your passport, left your
suitcase and your keys at home, your son has lost his glasses, your
daughters have lost their money and their tickets.
Report your troubles to the nearest sympathetic ear.

4 How would you tell someone that

1 last year your parents spent a week in Brighton, but this year they're
going to spend their holidays in Perpignan
2 your husband/wife didn't work yesterday, but he/she is going to the office
this morning

3 you've bought some postcards and some stamps, and you're going to write to your friends this afternoon

4 you and your husband/wife didn't do the shopping this morning, but you want to go to the hypermarket on Saturday

5 Listen to the cassette and underline the correct time.

(a) 6h16 16h06 10h16   (b) 9h30 19h30 10h30   (c) 12h30 00h30 12h00

6 Anne-Marie tells you how she spends a typical day. Pass on the information in French to your friends.

7 Your French friend is showing you three photos. What do you say about each one, starting with **il** or **elle**, and what do you really think about them?
1 wife 2 daughter 3 flat

1 charming / awful
2 beautiful / not very pretty
3 very beautiful / very old

Can you say it?   **Roland et Ivan sont des enfants fantastiques!** (Practise with the cassette)

KEY TO
CHECKPOINTS

1 1 J'ai mangé un sandwich à midi. 2 J'ai changé des travellers (chèques de voyage). 3 J'ai acheté des souvenirs. 4 Mes amis et moi, nous avons passé deux heures à Bordeaux. 5 Nous avons visité les caves.

2 Ils ont regardé la télé. Ils ont écouté des disques. Ils ont dansé. Ils ont joué au tennis.

3 (a) J'ai pris le bus (l'autobus), j'ai fait les courses, mais je n'ai pas vu Monique, j'ai visité le château, j'ai pris des photos, je n'ai pas écrit de lettres, j'ai fini mon travail, je n'ai pas regardé la télé. (b) Elle a pris . . . , elle a fait . . . , elle n'a pas vu . . . , elle a visité . . . , elle a pris . . . , elle n'a pas écrit . . . , elle a fini (son) . . . , elle n'a pas regardé . . .

4 L'année dernière Jacqueline n'est pas allée en Italie. 2 Cette année je suis allé(e) en Bretagne. 3 Ce matin, ma femme (mon mari) et moi, nous sommes allés au marché. 4 Dimanche, mes parents ne sont pas allés à la cathédrale. 5 Dimanche après-midi, Paul est allé au match.

5 Jacques est arrivé lundi. Il est parti mercredi. Il est resté trois jours. Marie-Claire est arrivée mardi. Elle est partie dimanche. Elle est restée six jours. Pierre et Charles sont arrivés jeudi. Ils sont partis dimanche. Ils sont restés quatre jours. Annick et Colette sont arrivées mardi. Elles sont parties samedi. Elles sont restées cinq jours. Mon père et moi, nous sommes arrivés jeudi. Nous sommes partis vendredi. Nous sommes restés deux jours.

6 Vendredi: Je suis arrivé(e) à Paris à dix heures. J'ai pris un taxi. Je suis allé(e) à l'hôtel. Samedi: Je suis allé(e) à Montmartre. J'ai mangé dans un petit café. L'après-midi j'ai pris le train. Je suis arrivé(e) à Versailles à trois heures et demie. Je suis allé(e) au château. J'ai visité les jardins. J'ai pris des photos. Dimanche: Le matin, je suis allé(e) au Jardin du Luxembourg. J'ai écrit dix cartes postales! J'ai passé l'après-midi à Fontainebleau.

Lundi: Jacques est venu à quatre heures. Le soir nous sommes allés au cinéma. Nous avons vu un bon film.

7 (a) 2 (b) 1 (c) 3

8 1 *to the Pyrénées*; 2 *great!* 3 *at a very pretty campsite*; 4 *no*; 5 *went out for walks and trips in the car*; 6 *to Provence (Nîmes)*; 7 *a fortnight*; 8 *very pleasant but rather expensive.*

KEY TO DOUBLE CHECKPOINTS

1 sont; sont; ont; ont; vont; font; vont.

2 Ils ont quel âge, vos enfants? Ils parlent anglais? Ils jouent au tennis? Ils font du ski nautique? Ils aiment sortir avec leurs ami(e)s anglais(es)?

3 J'ai oublié mon passeport, j'ai laissé ma valise et mes clés à la maison, mon fils a perdu ses lunettes, mes filles ont perdu leur argent et leurs billets.

4 1 L'année dernière mes parents ont passé une semaine (huit jours) à Brighton, mais cette année ils vont passer leurs vacances à Perpignan.
2 Mon mari (ma femme) n'a pas travaillé hier, mais il (elle) va au bureau ce matin. 3 J'ai acheté des cartes portales et des timbres, et je vais écrire à mes ami(e)s cet après-midi. 4 Mon mari (ma femme) et moi, nous n'avons pas fait les courses ce matin, mais nous voulons aller à l'hypermarché samedi.

5 (a) 16h06 (b) 9h30 (c) 00h30

6 Elle est secrétaire. A huit heures, elle prend le bus et elle va au bureau. A neuf heures, elle commence son travail. A midi trente elle va au restaurant avec ses collègues. A deux heures elle continue son travail. Elle finit à six heures et demie. Le soir, elle sort avec ses ami(e)s.

7 1 Elle est charmante (Elle est affreuse). 2 Elle est belle (Elle n'est pas très jolie). 3 Il est très beau (Il est très vieux).

▶ The next 11 chapters will give you practice in using French in the kind of situations you're likely to find yourself in when you're in France.

▶ You can work through the chapters in the order that suits you best.

▶ At the beginning of each chapter there's a checklist of the main language points you should look at again before going ahead. Numbers are important in each chapter, although this is not specifically mentioned in the checklists. There are also suggestions for extra practice.

▶ The section headed 'Basics' gives you words and expressions vital to the situations you're trying to cope with.

▶ In the conversations where you're asked to imitate one of the speakers, remember to use the pause button on your cassette recorder.

Food shopping

Food shops generally stay open till 7 or 8 p.m. Most have a long lunch break. They often close on Mondays but open on Sunday mornings. Markets in bigger towns are held most mornings, including Sunday. In small towns and villages there is a weekly market day (**le jour de marché**). In many markets you can buy dairy produce and meat.

Basics		
pour acheter . . . ?	where can I buy . . . ?
un peu	a little – to say what you want a little of, add **de**, e.g **un peu de fromage**, or say **un peu de ça** if you don' know the word for it
qu'est-ce que vous avez comme ... . ?	what sort of . . . do you have?
je voudrais	I'd like
c'est trop	that's too much
ça va?	is that all right?
un comme ça	one like that
et avec ça?	anything else?
c'est tout	that's all
un morceau	piece
une tranche	slice
un/une demi-. . .	half a . . . (e.g. **un demi-kilo**, **une demi-livre**)

Et avec ça?

11.1 **Where to buy what**

une boucherie Butcher's selling veal (**du veau**), beef (**du boeuf**), lamb (**d l'agneau**), pork (**du porc**) and sausages (**des saucisses**). You can often buy a chicken (**un poulet**) there. If it says **boucherie chevaline** or just **chevaline**, it means they sell only horsemeat.

une charcuterie Butcher's selling mainly porkmeats such as ham (**du jambon**), salami-type sausage (**du saucisson**, not **des saucisses**).

une rôtisserie, **un traiteur** These have no real equivalents in English. They sell a variety of prepared dishes, cooked meats and salads.

une boulangerie Baker's, often combined with **une pâtisserie** (pastry/cake shop). The most popular bread is **une baguette** (crusty French stick). A wholemeal loaf is **un pain complet**. Soft bread rolls are **des petits pains**. Pastries are **pâtisseries**.

une épicerie Grocer's, but the sign often says **alimentation** (foods) or sometimes just **libre-service** (self-service). They sell the usual range of groceries e.g. butter (**du beurre**), milk (**du lait**), bread (**du pain**), eggs (**des oeufs**), cheese (**du fromage**), washing powder (**de la lessive**). You can also buy apples (**des pommes**), potatoes (**des pommes de terre**), lettuce (**une laitue**), strawberries (**des fraises**), cherries (**des cerises**) etc. They generally stock drinks.

un marchand de vin Wine merchant, but the shop sign may say **cave** meaning wine cellar. In many you can buy local wine (**vin du pays**) straight from the barrel.

CHECKPOINT 1   There's no supermarket around. Say in French which shops sell

1 bread rolls   2 lamb chops   3 cooked meats   4 teabags
5 strawberries   6 strawberry tarts   7 bottle of Beaujolais

11.2 Buying groceries

S'il n'y a pas de supermarché dans le quartier, c'est le moment de faire un petit effort en français.

A l'épicerie Imitate the customer:

CLIENT   Je voudrais du beurre s'il vous plaît.
VENDEUSE Un paquet comme ça, voilà!
CLIENT   C'est trop. Un petit paquet s'il vous plaît. Qu'est-ce que vous avez comme fromage?
VENDEUSE Nous avons de tout. Qu'est-ce que je vous donne?
CLIENT   Un peu de gruyère.
VENDEUSE Vous voulez un morceau comme ça?
CLIENT   Ah non, c'est trop. Des tranches, s'il vous plaît. C'est pour notre pique-nique.

11.2 continued | VENDEUSE | Cent vingt grammes. Ça va? Oui? Et avec ça? Des fruits? Du vin? Des oeufs?* Du lait?
| CLIENT | Oui, un litre. Qu'est-ce que vous avez comme fruits?
| VENDEUSE | Fraises, cerises, melon, pêches, bananes . . .
| CLIENT | Elles sont bonnes, les cerises?
| VENDEUSE | Extra! Je vous donne un demi-kilo, cinq cents grammes?
| CLIENT | Une demi-livre. C'est tout. C'est combien?
| VENDEUSE | Ça vous fait . . . attendez . . . 29F90.
| CLIENT | Et pour acheter du pain?
| VENDEUSE | Il y a une boulangerie rue Marceau.

* **oeufs** rhymes with **deux**, but **oeuf** (sing.) rhymes with **neuf**

CHECKPOINT 2   Say in English what the customer bought and how much.

CHECKPOINT 3   How would you ask for: 1 a litre of milk   2 a piece of camembert   3 half a pound of butter   4 200 grams of ham   5 six eggs   6 a little of a delicious-looking cheese you don't know the name of!

Shopping for other things

Basics

vous avez	**autre chose?**	have you	anything else?
	plus grand/petit?		anything bigger/smaller?
	moins cher?		anything cheaper (i.e. less expensive)

c'est trop grand/petit/cher	that's too big/small/expensive
en coton/laine/cuir	made of cotton/wool/leather
je prends	I'll take
je peux essayer?	may I try . . . (on)?
les soldes m.pl.	sales

11.3 **Where to buy what**

une librairie Bookshop, not library. Often combined with **une papeterie** (stationer's). The sign may say **livres** (books) and **journaux** (papers).

la maison de la presse Sells all kinds of French and foreign newspapers and magazines. Also stocks books, maps and stationery.

un tabac Tobacconist's-cum-newsagent's. Also sells postcards (**des cartes postales**) and stamps (**des timbres**) to go with them. Often combined with a bar, **un bar-tabac**.

11.3 continued

une droguerie   Not a drugstore, but a place where you can get household goods and toiletries e.g. a toothbrush (**une brosse à dents**), soap (**du savon**), a comb (**un peigne**), suntan oil (**de l'huile pour bronzer**), tissues (**des kleenex**).

Vous avez de l'après-rasage?

une parfumerie   Sells mainly cosmetics and perfumes, and some toiletries such as after-shave (**de l'après-rasage**).

une pharmacie   Dispensing chemist's (21.3). Also sells a few toiletries.

Au tabac   Imitate the customer:

CLIENT   Vous avez des journaux anglais?

EMPLOYÉ   Américains, oui – anglais, non. Pour ça il faut aller à la maison de la presse. C'est à cinq minutes d'ici.

CLIENT   Ah bon. Alors, je prends trois cartes postales.

EMPLOYÉ   Trois cartes postales à un franc cinquante, ça fait quatre francs cinquante. Vous voulez aussi des timbres?

CLIENT   Oui, s'il vous plaît, un pour l'Angleterre, un pour l'Irlande et un pour les Etats-Unis, par avion.

EMPLOYÉ   Voilà! Ça fait six francs cinq centimes. C'est tout?

CLIENT   Merci, c'est tout.

CHECKPOINT 4   Complete your side of the conversation at the **droguerie**.

VOUS   *(say you'd like a toothbrush)*

VENDEUSE   Dur ou souple?

VOUS   *(hard, please)*

VENDEUSE   Comme ça? Ça coûte huit francs.

VOUS   *(say you'd like some suntan oil)*

VENDEUSE   Voilà! Autre chose? Du savon? Du shampooing? Des kleenex?

VOUS   *(ask if they have any after-shave)*

VENDEUSE   Non, pour ça, il faut aller à la parfumerie.

CHECKPOINT 5   Listen to the cassette and give the name of the shop (in French) where each conversation takes place.

For groups   Tell your partner (in French) what you want to buy. He/she will tell you which shop you have to go to.

11.4 **Buying something to wear**

Some of the things you may want to buy are a jumper (**un pull**), a pair of trousers (**un pantalon**), a shirt (**une chemise**), a swim-suit (**un maillot de bain**), a pair of tights (**un collant**), shoes (**des chaussures**), a sun-dress (**une robe bain de soleil**).

C'est trop petit!

Quelle pointure? means 'what size shoes?'. Size 5 = 38, size 6 = 39 etc.
Quelle taille? means 'what size?' when you're buying clothes. Women's size 14 is usually **taille 42**, size 16 is **taille 44** etc.
But your best answer to **quelle taille? quelle pointure?** may be **je ne sais pas**, and let the shop assistant work it out.

Dans un grand magasin   Imitate the customer:

CLIENTE	Je voudrais un pull marron.
VENDEUSE	J'ai des pulls en laine et en coton pur.
CLIENTE	En coton, s'il vous plaît.
VENDEUSE	Et quelle taille?
CLIENT	Je ne sais pas.
VENDEUSE	Essayez le 42. Voilà un beau pull en coton pur.
CLIENTE	C'est combien, le pull?
VENDEUSE	195F.
CLIENTE	Vous avez moins cher?
VENDEUSE	Oui, il y a des pulls en solde, mais pas en marron.
CLIENTE	Bon alors, je peux essayer le pull à 195F?
VENDEUSE	Bien sûr, madame.

CHECKPOINT 6

1 Say you'd like grey cotton trousers.
2 Ask if they have anything cheaper.
3 Say you'd like a green shirt for your son.
4 Ask where you can buy a swim-suit.

CHECKPOINT 7   Listen to the conversation in a shoeshop, then answer the questions.

1 What size did the customer want?
2 What size was she shown?
3 What were the shoes made of?
4 Were they too big, too small or just right?
5 How much were the leather ones?

11.5 Hunting for souvenirs and presents

When you buy a present (**un cadeau**), they usually ask **je vous fais un paquet-cadeau?** (shall I gift-wrap it for you?). If not, tell them it's for a present (**c'est pour offrir**).

Dans un magasin de cadeaux-souvenirs   Imitate the customer. Try to guess what **une poupée** and **un bol** are, then check with the word list.

CLIENTE	Je cherche un petit cadeau pour ma nièce.
VENDEUSE	Oui. Elle a quel âge?
CLIENTE	Elle a douze ans.
VENDEUSE	Eh bien, nous avons des poupées en costume régional qui sont très jolies.
CLIENTE	Elle n'aime pas les poupées.
VENDEUSE	Ah bon! Alors, quelque chose en poterie? Un joli petit bol avec son nom dessus. Comment s'appelle-t-elle?
CLIENTE	Jane. C'est un nom anglais.

VENDEUSE Je regrette, mais nous n'avons pas de bols avec ce nom. Mmm . . . pour une fillette de douze ans . . . un petit bracelet? Ça fait toujours plaisir!

CLIENTE C'est combien?

VENDEUSE Le petit bracelet en argent, ça coûte 148F. Nous avons moins cher, à 55F, mais ils ne sont pas en argent.

CLIENTE Bon, je prends le bracelet en argent.

VENDEUSE Je vous fais un paquet-cadeau?

CHECKPOINT 8 | True or false? Re-read the conversation first.

1 La cliente a acheté une poupée pour sa nièce.
2 Sa nièce adore les poupées.
3 Il n'y a pas de bols avec le nom de sa nièce.
4 La cliente prend le bracelet en argent.

For groups | Discuss what presents you're going to buy for everyone, and say where you're going to get them.

Can you say it? | **un petit pantalon blanc en coton** (Practise with the cassette)

KEY TO CHECKPOINTS

1 1 une boulangerie; 2 une boucherie; 3 une charcuterie, une rôtisserie, un traiteur; 4 une épicerie; 5 une épicerie; 6 une pâtisserie; 7 un marchand de vin, une épicerie.

2 *a small packet of butter, 120gr of gruyère slices, a litre of milk, half a pound of cherries.*

3 1 un litre de lait; 2 un morceau de camembert; 3 une demi-livre de beurre; 4 deux cents grammes de jambon; 5 six oeufs; 6 un peu de ça!

4 VOUS: Je voudrais une brosse à dents . . . Dur, s'il vous plaît . . . Je voudrais de l'huile pour bronzer . . . Vous avez de l'après-rasage?

5 1 un tabac; 2 une librairie (la maison de la presse); 3 une parfumerie.

6 1 Je voudrais un pantalon gris en coton. 2 Vous avez moins cher? 3 Je voudrais une chemise verte pour mon fils. 4 Pour acheter un maillot de bain?

7 1 *size 38*; 2 *size 37*; 3 *plastic*; 4 *too small*; 5 *170F*.

8 1 *false*; 2 *false*; 3 *true*; 4 *true*.

Hotel accommodation

Basics

	un hôtel deux (trois etc) étoiles	two (three etc)-star hotel
	une auberge	inn
	c'est complet	it's full, fully booked
une chambre	**pour une personne**	single room
	pour deux personnes	double room
	à deux lits	room with twin beds
	avec grand lit	room with double bed
avec	**cabinet m. de toilette**	with basin and bidet partitioned off
	salle f. de bains	with bathroom
	douche f./bain m./WC m.	with shower/bath/WC
	(**WC** sounds a bit like 'vay-say')	
	avec pension f. complète	with full board (**une pension** is a boarding house)
	pour combien de nuits/personnes?	for how many nights/people?
	la salle à manger	dining room
	le petit déjeuner	breakfast
	ça vous va?	is that suitable?

C'est une auberge une étoile!

12.1 **Looking for a hotel**

The local tourist office (**l'office de tourisme** or **le syndicat d'initiative**) will help you find a hotel. Charges are usually per room, not per person, and don't always include breakfast.

A l'office de tourisme   Imitate the tourist:

TOURISTE   Bonjour. Je cherche une chambre.
HÔTESSE   Une chambre dans un hôtel ou une chambre à louer?

TOURISTE	Dans un hôtel.
HÔTESSE	Pour combien de personnes?
TOURISTE	C'est pour ma femme et moi.
HÔTESSE	Et pour combien de nuits?
TOURISTE	Pour trois nuits.
HÔTESSE	Un instant, je vais téléphoner . . . Je peux réserver une chambre à l'Hôtel Victoria. C'est un hôtel deux étoiles.
TOURISTE	C'est combien, la chambre?
HÔTESSE	Le prix de la chambre, avec grand lit et cabinet de toilette, est de cent vingt francs, taxes et service compris.
TOURISTE	Le petit déjeuner est compris?
HÔTESSE	Ah non, c'est dix-huit francs par personne. Ça vous va?
TOURISTE	Oui, très bien, merci.

CHECKPOINT 1

Underline the correct answer.

1 The man wants a room for 1 person/2 people/3 people
2 The room he is offered has a bath/basin & bidet/shower/WC
3 The price of the room is 80F/180F/120F
4 It includes service/breakfast/evening meal
5 It's a 1-star/2-star/3-star hotel

12.2 **Asking for rooms**

Don't be misled – not every **hôtel** provides accommodation!

A l'hôtel   Imitate the tourist:

TOURISTE	Bonsoir. Vous avez une chambre pour le weekend?
RÉCEPTIONNISTE	Je peux vous donner une belle chambre au premier étage avec terrasse et salle de bains. C'est une chambre avec grand lit. Ça vous va?
TOURISTE	Non, je préfère une chambre à deux lits.
RÉCEPTIONNISTE	Alors, j'ai une petite chambre au quatrième étage. C'est une chambre à deux lits, avec douche et WC.

TOURISTE	C'est combien, la chambre?
RÉCEPTIONNISTE	Cent dix francs, taxes et service compris. Ça vous va?
TOURISTE	D'accord! Ça va très bien.

CHECKPOINT 2　　Take part in this conversation at the hotel.

VOUS	*(say good evening and ask if they have a room)*
RÉCEPTIONNISTE	Oui, qu'est-ce que vous voulez comme chambre? Une chambre pour une personne?
VOUS	*(no, a double room – a quiet room)*
RÉCEPTIONNISTE	C'est pour combien de nuits?
VOUS	*(for four nights)*
RÉCEPTIONNISTE	Oui, j'ai une chambre avec salle de bains.
VOUS	*(ask how much it is)*
RÉCEPTIONNISTE	160F.
VOUS	*(ask if that's with full board)*
RÉCEPTIONNISTE	Non, c'est le prix de la chambre avec petit déjeuner.

CHECKPOINT 3　　Listen to the cassette and answer the questions.

1　Do they have a room?
2　Is there likely to be one in the area?
3　What advice does the receptionist offer?
4　Where is the tourist office?

12.3 **Checking in**

A la réception　　Imitate the hotel guest:

CLIENT	Bonjour, nous avons réservé une chambre.
PATRON	A quel nom, s'il vous plaît?
CLIENT	Monsieur et Madame Clements.
PATRON	Ah oui, vous êtes dans la chambre deux cent treize. C'est une chambre avec grand lit, bain et WC. C'est au deuxième étage. Vous avez des bagages?
CLIENT	Oui, ils sont dans la voiture.
PATRON	On va vous les monter tout de suite.
CLIENT	Je peux laisser la voiture dans la rue?
PATRON	Ah non, il y a un parking à côté de l'hôtel.
CLIENT	Bon! C'est à quelle heure, le petit déjeuner?

PATRON   Quand vous voulez, jusqu'à dix heures. Vous pouvez prendre le petit déjeuner dans votre chambre ou dans la salle à manger, comme vous voulez.

CHECKPOINT 4   Right or wrong? Check with the previous conversation.

1 The guests have room 215
2 They have a room with a shower
3 They have a room with a double bed
4 Breakfast is served until 11 o'clock
5 Their luggage is in the car
6 There's a car park next to the hotel

12.4 Complaining

The most common complaints usually begin **il n'y a pas de (d')** . . . there isn't/aren't any . . . Or it may be a matter of something not working, . . . **ne marche/marchent pas.**

Maman, la douche ne marche pas —

— et il n'y a pas d'eau chaude!

CHECKPOINT 5   The Hôtel Splendide doesn't live up to its name. How do you say

1 the shower doesn't work
2 there's no hot water
3 there's no towel in your room
4 there are no blankets
5 the lamps don't work
6 you'd like to speak to the manager

For groups   (a) Read the conversations again with a partner, taking turns to be the tourist/hotel guest, and eventually memorising what he/she says.

(b) See who can think up the most hair-raising set of complaints about a hotel you're staying in.

Camping

Basics

camper	to camp	**un emplacement**	pitch
un camping	campsite	**une tente**	tent
le bloc sanitaire	washing facilities	**une caravane**	caravan

12.5 Looking for a campsite

The local tourist office has lists of campsites. They can also tell you where you're likely to get in. They may be able to help you book in during the peak periods. Spots that look inviting for camping often have the sign **camping interdit** (no camping)!

Sur la route   Imitate the tourist:

TOURISTE	Pardon monsieur, on peut camper ici?
HOMME	Non, c'est interdit. C'est privé.
TOURISTE	Il y a un camping par ici?
HOMME	Oui, il y a un camping à cinq kilomètres d'ici.
TOURISTE	C'est un bon camping?
HOMME	Oui, monsieur, c'est un camping trois étoiles avec douches, piscine etc. C'est pas mal!

CHECKPOINT 6   Summarise in English the information the tourist is given.

12.6 Arriving at the campsite   Si vous n'avez pas de carnet de camping international il est possible qu'on vous demande de payer à l'arrivée et de laisser votre passeport au bureau.

Au camping   Imitate the camper:

CAMPEUR	Vous avez un emplacement pour une tente?
EMPLOYÉ	Oui, j'ai un emplacement. Voilà les tarifs. Vous restez combien de jours?
CAMPEUR	Je ne sais pas. Je peux rester une semaine?
EMPLOYÉ	Oui, si vous voulez. Votre passeport, s'il vous plaît.
CAMPEUR	J'ai un carnet de camping international.
EMPLOYÉ	Alors, vous payez quand vous partez.
CAMPEUR	Où est le bloc sanitaire, s'il vous plaît?
EMPLOYÉ	Il y a deux blocs sanitaires, tous les deux avec eau chaude. Ils sont là-bas.
CAMPEUR	Très bien. Je peux téléphoner?
EMPLOYÉ	Oui, il y a une cabine téléphonique à côté du restaurant.
CAMPEUR	Merci bien!

CHECKPOINT 7   Listen to the cassette and complete these sentences.

1 Vous êtes . . . . . . personnes?
2 Ma femme et moi et . . . enfants.
3 C'est . . . F pour les deux adultes et . . . F pour chaque enfant.
4 Il y a des douches . . . ?
5 Vous avez aussi une . . . ?
6 Vous voulez un . . . ?
7 Vous . . . combien de jours?

CHECKPOINT 8   Your camping guide says the campsite has the following facilities – ask where they are: 1 showers   2 toilets   3 shops   4 supermarket   5 swimming pool   6 petrol station

Writing letters

12.7 Writing to the tourist office

Monsieur,

J'ai l'intention de visiter Nice au mois de juillet.
Voulez-vous être assez aimable de m'envoyer une liste des hôtels et des campings et aussi des brochures sur la ville et ses environs.

Je vous prie, monsieur, d'agréer l'expression de mes sentiments distingués ...

Dear Sir,

I intend to visit Nice during the month of July.
Please would you be kind enough to send me a list of hotels and campsites, and also some brochures on the town and surroundings.

Yours faithfully, ...

12.8 Booking accommodation

Monsieur,

Vous serait-il possible de nous réserver une chambre à 2 lits avec douche pour les nuits du 5 au 7 juin inclus?
Je vous serais reconnaissant(e) de bien vouloir m'indiquer vos prix.

En vous remerciant d'avance, je vous prie, etc (as above)

Dear Sir,

Would it be possible for you to reserve us a twin-bedded room with shower for the nights of 5-7 June inclusive?
I should be grateful if you would be kind enough to let me know your charges.

Thanking you in anticipation, yours faithfully, ...

KEY TO CHECKPOINTS

1 1 *two people*; 2 *basin and bidet*; 3 *120F*; 4 *service*; 5 *2-star*.

2 VOUS: Bonsoir. Vous avez une chambre? . . . Non, une chambre pour deux personnes, une chambre tranquille . . . Pour quatre nuits . . . C'est combien? . . . C'est avec pension complète?

3 1 *no*; 2 *no*; 3 *ask at the tourist office*; 4 *opposite the town hall.*

4 1 *wrong (room 213)*; 2 *wrong (with bath & WC)*; 3 *right*; 4 *wrong (until 10)*; 5 *right*; 6 *right.*

5 1 La douche ne marche pas. 2 Il n'y a pas d'eau chaude. 3 Il n'y a pas de serviette dans ma (notre) chambre. 4 Il n'y a pas de couvertures. 5 Les lampes ne marchent pas. 6 Je voudrais parler au patron.

6 *No camping allowed here – private property. There's a campsite 5km away, 3-star site with showers, swimming pool etc.*

7 1 combien de; 2 deux; 3 40, 10; 4 chaudes; 5 piscine; 6 emplacement; 7 restez.

8 1 Où sont les douches? 2 Où sont les toilettes? 3 Où sont les magasins? 4 Où est le supermarché? 5 Où est la piscine? 6 Où est la station-service?

CHECKLIST

saying what you want (2.1, 7.6)
going into details (3.1, 4.6)
asking what's available (2.6, 4.3)
stating preferences, likes and dislikes (7.1, 7.4)
'some' and 'any' (2.8, 2.7, 6.5)

MENU TERMS

To help you understand what's on the menu, there's an alphabetical list of food and drink at the back.

Basics

on mange bien	the food's good (lit. one eats well)
le menu	set meal (but the menu is **la carte**)
l'addition f.	bill
le plat du jour	today's special
bon appétit!	enjoy your meal!
à votre santé!	cheers! (the reply is **à la vôtre!**)
commander	to order
qu'est-ce que vous avez comme . . . ?	what kind of . . . do you have?
boire	to drink
la boisson	drink
compris	included
conseiller	to recommend
encore du/de la . . . etc	some more . . .
la cuisine	food or cooking (also means kitchen)
saignant/bleu	underdone, very rare
à point	medium
bien cuit	well done
il n'y a plus de . . .	there's no more . . .

13.1 **Looking for somewhere to eat**

Set meals range from the modest **menu touristique** to the pricey **menu gastronomique**. Most eating places close one day a week.
Un restaurant is not the only place for a meal. Try one of these:

un bar   Serves drinks, coffee, light breakfast and often snacks. Usually open from early morning till late.

une brasserie   A cross between a café and a restaurant, offering snacks and a limited range of dishes at any time.

le buffet de la gare   More like a restaurant. Food is usually good.

une crêperie   A pancake house serving sweet and savoury pancakes. They're a speciality of Brittany.

un relais routier   A roadside restaurant for lorry drivers and also hungry tourists who want value for money. They serve set meals, often with drink included (**boisson comprise**).

A l'hôtel   Imitate the tourist:

	TOURISTE	Il y a un bon restaurant par ici?
	RÉCEPTIONNISTE	Oui, vous avez la Belle Etoile au coin de la rue.
	TOURISTE	C'est cher?
	RÉCEPTIONNISTE	Oui, un peu. Vous préférez quelque chose de plus simple, de plus typique? Une crêperie? Une brasserie?
	TOURISTE	Un petit restaurant typique.
	RÉCEPTIONNISTE	Il faut aller au port. Là vous avez des restaurants dans tous les prix. Vous aimez la cuisine régionale? Vous voulez manger des plats typiques?
	TOURISTE	Oui, nous préférons manger des plats typiques.
	RÉCEPTIONNISTE	Eh bien, je vous conseille d'aller au Petit Cochon.
	TOURISTE	On mange bien au Petit Cochon?
	RÉCEPTIONNISTE	Très bien, et ce n'est pas cher. C'est une ambiance très sympathique.

CHECKPOINT 1   How do you ask if   1 there's a roadside restaurant around   2 the food is good   3 it's far   4 it's expensive

13.2 Sitting down to a meal

Mais chéri, je ne mange pas de poisson!

To call the waiter say **monsieur!** In a café or bar you say **garçon!** The waitress is **mademoiselle** even if she's on the mature side.

Au Petit Cochon   Imitate the tourist:

	TOURISTE	Vous avez une table pour une personne?
	GARÇON	Oui monsieur. Il y a une place là-bas . . . Voilà la carte, monsieur . . . Eh bien, qu'est-ce que vous prenez?
	TOURISTE	Qu'est-ce que vous conseillez?
	GARÇON	Prenez le plat du jour. C'est une bouillabaisse.
	TOURISTE	Qu'est-ce que c'est, une bouillabaisse?
	GARÇON	C'est une soupe faite avec des poissons. C'est très bon.

13.2 continued

une boisson

un poisson

du poison

TOURISTE	Ah non, je n'aime pas ça!
GARÇON	Alors vous préférez la viande? Je vous conseille le menu à 58F. Pour commencer, oeuf mayonnaise ou pâté. Puis poulet rôti ou gigot d'agneau.
TOURISTE	Très bien. Le menu à 58F. Un pâté, puis le gigot.
GARÇON	Et comme boisson? Une bouteille de rouge?
TOURISTE	Une demi-bouteille et de l'eau minérale.
GARÇON	Très bien. *(later)* C'était bon?
TOURISTE	Très bon, merci. Qu'est-ce que vous avez comme dessert?
GARÇON	Fromage, glace vanille, tarte aux fraises, yaourt.
TOURISTE	Je prends du fromage. Et un café noir. *(later)* Monsieur, l'addition, s'il vous plaît.

CHECKPOINT 2

How would you

1 call the waiter/waitress
2 ask for the set meal at 55F
3 say you don't like meat

4 ask what sort of wine they have
5 ask for a good bottle of red wine
6 ask the waiter what he recommends

13.2 continued

A la Belle Etoile Imitate the customers:

GARÇON	Alors messieurs-dames, vous avez choisi?
MONSIEUR	Oui, nous avons choisi. Pour commencer, un cocktail de crevettes pour madame et des huîtres pour moi.
GARÇON	Très bien. Et ensuite?
MONSIEUR	Ensuite, pour madame, une sole. N'est-ce pas, chérie?
GARÇON	Je regrette, il n'y a plus de sole.
MADAME	Bon alors, je prends une escalope de veau.
MONSIEUR	Et pour moi, un steak.
GARÇON	Vous le voulez comment, votre steak – saignant, à point ou bien cuit?
MONSIEUR	Bien cuit, s'il vous plaît.
GARÇON	Et qu'est-ce que vous prenez comme légumes?
MONSIEUR	Nous prenons des petits pois.
MADAME	Ah non, pour moi, des épinards et du riz.
MONSIEUR	Et des frites pour moi. Et comme boisson, une bouteille de rosé.

GARÇON (*after the first course*) Voilà messieurs-dames! Une escalope pour madame et un steak pour monsieur. Petits pois, épinards et frites. Bon appétit!

MONSIEUR Et le riz?

GARÇON Le riz?

MONSIEUR Oui, madame a commandé du riz.

GARÇON Je m'excuse, monsieur. Je vous l'apporte tout de suite.

MADAME Et encore du pain, s'il vous plaît.

GARÇON Oui, madame, tout de suite madame.

CHECKPOINT 3
Re-read the conversation, and say what the customer and his wife had to eat and drink.

CHECKPOINT 4
What is the waiter saying?

1a Do you want the fish course?
b What will you have to drink?
c What would you like to follow?

2a There are no more vegetables
b Have you ordered vegetables?
c What vegetables will you have?

3a How would you like your steak?
b There's no more steak left
c Would you prefer steak?

4a Do you prefer yogurt?
b What sort of yogurt do you like?
c There isn't any more yogurt

CHECKPOINT 5
These things should be on the table at the start of your meal:

1 pain m.
2 huile f.
3 vinaigre m.
4 sel m.
5 poivre m.
6 moutarde f.
7 verre m.
8 couteau m.
9 cuillère f.
10 fourchette f.
11 serviette f.

Your waiter is very forgetful. How would you

1 ask for a small spoon
2 say you haven't a knife
3 ask if he has any mustard
4 ask for some salt and pepper
5 ask if there's any oil and vinegar
6 ask if he has any bread
7 say you haven't a napkin
8 say you haven't a glass

For groups
(a) Using the conversations in 13.1 and 13.2 as a guide, act out similar situations varying the dishes by consulting the list at the back.

(b) Try this memory game with the names of things on the meal table. See how many correct items can be reeled off before memory fails.
1st person: **Je voudrais du pain.** 2nd person adds an item: **Je voudrais du pain et de l'eau.** 3rd person adds another item, and so on.

For fun!   (a) What's the message?

My first is in Burgundy, Beaujolais, Beaune.
My second (like water?) a drink from the Rhône?
In **vin blanc** and **cognac** you'll find my third.
My fourth starts the alphabet, also this word.
My fifth is in **petits** and also in **pois**,
My sixth is in **pâté**, but never in **foie**.
My next begins spinach, not English but French.
The following letter British thirsts will quench!
The next one in French bread and wine you will see,
At the end of **dessert** my last one will be.
My whole, on the whole, is rarely said here,
But in France, when they say it, it brings good cheer.

(b) The word in the vertical box tells you where to go for quick meal.

1 Une . . . de Beaujolais
2 Nous . . . le menu à 48F
3 Le . . . du jour
4 La . . . est comprise?
5 La . . . de poissons
6 Qu'est-ce que vous . . . ?
7 Vous aimez la cuisine . . . ?
8 Et comme dessert, une . . .
9 On . . . bien?

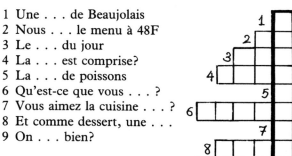

KEY TO
CHECKPOINTS

1 1 Il y a un relais routier par ici? 2 On mange bien? 3 C'est loin? 4 C'est cher?

2 1 Monsieur! (Garçon!) Mademoiselle! 2 Le menu à cinquante-cinq francs. 3 Je n'aime pas la viande. 4 Qu'est-ce que vous avez comme vin? 5 Une bonne bouteille de vin rouge. 6 Qu'est-ce que vous conseillez?

3 *man: oysters, steak (well done), peas, French fries, rosé wine.*
woman: prawn cocktail, veal cutlet, spinach, rice, rosé wine, bread.

4 1b 2c 3b 4a.

5 1 Une petite cuillère svp. 2 Je n'ai pas de couteau. 3 Vous avez de la moutarde? 4 Du sel et du poivre svp. 5 Il y a de l'huile et du vinaigre? 6 Vous avez du pain? 7 Je n'ai pas de serviette. 8 Je n'ai pas de verre.

For fun! (a) Bon appétit! (b) 1 bouteille; 2 prenons; 3 plat; 4 boisson; 5 soupe; 6 conseillez; 7 régionale; 8 pâtisserie; 9 mange.
The word in the vertical box is brasserie.

CHECKLIST

finding out what's around (4.3)
asking the way (5.2)
understanding directions (5.5)
asking about times and prices (4.5, 4.8, 4.9)
days of the week (10.2)

EXTRA PRACTICE

chapter 4 checkpoint 11
chapter 5 checkpoint 6
chapter 16 (16.7)

Basics		
	le syndicat d'initiative	tourist office
	des renseignements m.pl.	information
	qu'est-ce qu'il y a à voir?	what is there to see?
	qu'est-ce qu'il y a comme . . . ?	what sort of . . . is/are there?
	un plan de la ville	town map
	les vieux quartiers m.pl.	old part of the town
	les monuments m.pl.	important buildings (sometimes monuments)
	le musée des beaux-arts	museum of fine arts, art gallery
	une exposition	exhibition
	une visite guidée	guided tour
	faire une excursion	to go on an excursion/trip
	un autocar, un car	coach (not a car)
	l'entrée f.	way in, also admission charge
	la sortie	way out
	se trouve(nt)	is/are situated

14.1 **Finding out what to see**

Demandez des renseignements à l'office de tourisme ou au syndicat d'initiative. Demandez aussi des brochures sur la ville et les environs, et un plan de la ville. Si vous voulez écrire à l'avance, consultez les lettres au chapitre 12 (12.7).

Au syndicat d'initiative   Imitate the tourist:

TOURISTE   Bonjour. Vous avez un plan de la ville, s'il vous plaît?
HÔTESSE   Oui madame.
TOURISTE   Qu'est-ce qu'il y a à voir? Nous ne connaissons pas Lyon.

HÔTESSE	Alors, je vous conseille de visiter un peu la vieille ville. Les vieux quartiers sont très intéressants.
TOURISTE	Qu'est-ce qu'il y a comme monuments?
HÔTESSE	Ils sont marqués sur le plan. Ici vous avez la cathédrale St Jean, et ici . . .
TOURISTE	C'est loin, la cathédrale?
HÔTESSE	Non, c'est à dix minutes à pied. Vous traversez la place Bellecour, une des plus grandes d'Europe. Ensuite vous traversez le pont Bonaparte et vous arrivez tout de suite dans les vieux quartiers.
TOURISTE	Et qu'est-ce qu'il y a pour les enfants?
HÔTESSE	Vous avez le Musée International de la Marionnette, ou bien le Musée de l'Automobile qui se trouve à douze kilomètres d'ici. Ça fait toujours plaisir aux enfants.
TOURISTE	Et aussi à mon mari!

CHECKPOINT 1

How do you ask

1 for a town map
2 what there is to see
3 what sort of important buildings there are
4 if it's far to the old town
5 what there is for the children
6 where the town hall is

14.2 **Visiting places of interest**

Museums are generally open every day except Tuesday. On one day a week, admission (**entrée**) is sometimes free (**gratuit**). When you're sightseeing, check whether places of interest are open on public holidays (**fêtes** or **jours fériés**). Some may close for lunch.

This is the kind of information you may find about places of interest:

Azay-le-Rideau

Le plus féminin des châteaux de la Loire. Les grandes salles du château offrent de très beaux meubles, tableaux et tapisseries. Avril-septembre tous les jours de 9h15 à 12h et de 14h à 18h30. Prix d'entrée 13F. Etudiants de 18 à 25 ans (avec carte) 6F50. Dimanches et fêtes demi-tarif.

Arc de Triomphe

Construit au 19e siècle en l'honneur des armées françaises. Intérieur et plate-forme de l'arc: accès tous les jours de 10h à 17h30. Belle vue sur Paris. Prix: 12F en semaine, 6F le dimanche.

┌───┐
│ ─────────────**Musée des Beaux-Arts**───────────── │
│ *Tous les jours sauf mardi de 9h à 12h et de 14h à 18h. Peintures,* │
│ *sculptures, antiquités, tapisseries. Exposition de peintures* │
│ *contemporaines. Entrée 3F. Dimanche gratuit.* │
└───┘

CHECKPOINT 2   You want to visit the places of interest in 14.2.

1 Which are closed on Tuesdays?
2 Which are closed for lunch?
3 Which is generally the best day to visit if you're hard up?
4 Which holds most interest for modern art buffs?

CHECKPOINT 3   (a) Ask how to get to the places in 14.2.
                (b) Note down in English the directions you're given on cassette.

CHECKPOINT 4   The two of you and your 12-year-old daughter want to visit the castle. Fill in your part of the conversation.

EMPLOYÉ   Vous prenez vos billets ici à la caisse.
VOUS   *(ask how much the admission charge is)*
EMPLOYÉ   L'entrée est de cinq francs par personne.
VOUS   *(ask for three tickets please)*
EMPLOYÉ   L'enfant a quel âge?
VOUS   *(say how old she is)*
EMPLOYÉ   Alors c'est gratuit pour la petite. Ça fait dix francs.
VOUS   *(ask if there's a guided tour)*
EMPLOYÉ   Oui, dans deux minutes. Vous attendez le guide ici.

14.3 Understanding the guide

The kind of English your guide speaks may not be easy to understand!

So try to get the gist of what he says in French. These are some of the key words and phrases which are usually in the guide's 'patter':

le roi, la reine	king, queen
sous le règne de . . .	in the reign of . . .
au Moyen Age	in the Middle Ages
pendant la guerre	during the war
au dix-septième siècle	in the 17th century (**siècle** may be omitted)

(re)construit, détruit	(re)built, destroyed
achevé	completed
brûlé	burnt
les tableaux m.pl.	pictures, paintings
les vitraux m.pl.	stained-glass windows
le chef-d'oeuvre	masterpiece
la tour	tower

CHECKPOINT 5   This is what your guide tells you when you visit (a) the castle (b) the cathedral. Summarise the details for the benefit of your non-French-speaking friends.

14.4 Coping with dates

The guide may well bombard you with dates. Here's how they're given:

en	quinze seize dix-sept dix-neuf	cent	trente quarante deux quatre-vingt-six	in	1530 1640 1702 1986

From the 1700s onwards, dates may also be given like this:

en	mil	sept huit neuf	cent	deux soixante-et-onze quatre-vingt-six	in	1702 1871 1986

In dates, you write **mil** (thousand), not **mille** (pronounced the same).

CHECKPOINT 6   Listen to the cassette and fill in the dates in figures.

(a) Ce chef-d'oeuvre de style flamboyant a été construit en . . .
(b) L'église a été commencée en . . . et achevée en . . .
(c) Les vieux quartiers ont été détruits en . . .
(d) La tour a été construite en . . . sous le règne de Louis XIV
(e) Jeanne d'Arc a été brûlée par les Anglais en . . .

For groups

Discuss with your partner the places of interest in your area, and how to get to them. Then try talking about places in other towns.

14.5 Going on an excursion

You can book excursions at a travel agent's (**une agence de voyages**). You'll often find one at main railway stations.

These are the kind of details you might read about sightseeing trips. Don't be misled – **journée** means whole day, never journey.

BEAUNE journée Prestigieuse cité du vin. Musée du vin. Visite d'une cave. Dégustation gratuite. *Dimanche départ* 7h *Retour vers* 23h30 **40F**	**GRASSE** journée Cité provençale d'art et d'histoire. Centre mondial de la parfumerie et de la fabrication des huiles aromatiques essentielles. Station réputée. Sa campagne, ses fleurs, ses vieilles rues, sa cathédrale du XIIe siècle. Beau panorama. A visiter: les parfumeries **56F**
CHARTRES après-midi La cathédrale – ses statues – ses vitraux – sa crypte. Promenade dans la vieille ville médiévale. *Dimanches et fêtes* **34F**	

CHECKPOINT 7

Deux places, s'il vous plaît

(a) Say briefly in English what the attractions are of each place in 14.5.

(b) You and your friend decide to book a trip to Chartres. Speak for both of you.

VOUS (*say you'd like to go on an excursion to Chartres*)
EMPLOYÉ Vous voulez réserver des places pour aujourd'hui?
VOUS (*say no, you'd like to book two seats for tomorrow*)
EMPLOYÉ Deux places pour demain. Très bien. Ça vous fait 68F.
VOUS (*ask if the coach leaves from here*)
EMPLOYÉ Oui, vous partez d'ici à 13h30.
VOUS (*ask when it arrives*)
EMPLOYÉ Vers deux heures et demie.
VOUS (*ask if there's a guide*)
EMPLOYÉ Bien sûr! C'est un jeune étudiant qui s'appelle Achille.
VOUS (*ask if he speaks English*)

N'oubliez pas le guide!

For groups | Exchange travellers' tales. Talk about what you saw and did on a sightseeing trip, real or imaginary. First have another look at chapter 10 to remind yourself how to talk about the past.

CHECKPOINT 8 | ✉ What's in store for you at the end of your visit to the wine cellars?

KEY TO CHECKPOINTS

1 1 Un plan de la ville, svp. 2 Qu'est-ce qu'il y a à voir? 3 Qu'est-ce qu'il y a comme monuments? 4 C'est loin, la vieille ville? (La vieille ville, c'est loin?) 5 Qu'est-ce qu'il y a pour les enfants? 6 Où est l'hôtel de ville (la mairie)?

2 1 Musée des Beaux-Arts; 2 Azay-le-Rideau, Musée des Beaux-Arts; 3 *Sunday*; 4 Musée des Beaux Arts.

3 (a) Pour aller à Azay-le-Rideau? Pour aller à l'Arc de Triomphe? Pour aller au Musée des Beaux-Arts?

(b) Azay-le-Rideau: *Take the 1st road on the left, then carry straight on. When you get to the town centre, ask.*

Arc de Triomphe: *Go up this street, take the 2nd right which takes you straight to the Avenue des Champs Elysées. The Arc de Triomphe is on your left.*

Musée des Beaux-Arts: *Take the 14 bus as far as the town hall, then go up the rue Wilson, and take the 1st turning on the right.*

4 VOUS: C'est combien, l'entrée? (L'entrée, c'est combien?) . . . Trois billets, svp . . . Elle a douze ans . . . Il y a une visite guidée?

5 (a) *Dates back to the Middle Ages. Was destroyed during the Hundred Years War. Rebuilt in the 18th century and was a military hospital during the occupation.*

(b) *Begun in the 10th century, completed in the 13th century. The chapel is a masterpiece of Gothic architecture. Built in the reign of Charles V. Magnificent 14th-century stained-glass windows.*

6 (a) 1343   (b) 1173, 1251   (c) 1942   (d) 1699   (e) 1431.

7 (a) Beaune: *wine museum, visit to a wine cellar, free wine tasting.*   Chartres: *cathedral with statues, stained glass and crypt, walk through the old town dating back to the Middle Ages.*   Grasse: *world centre for manufacture of perfume. Renowned resort. Countryside, flowers, old streets, 12th-century cathedral. Beautiful view. Perfumeries worth visiting.*

(b) VOUS: Nous voulons faire une excursion à Chartres . . . Non, nous voulons réserver deux places pour demain . . . L'autocar (le car) part d'ici? . . . Il arrive quand? . . . Il y a un guide? . . . Il parle anglais?

8 *A glass of wine and the possibility of buying bottles of wine at a special price, followed by a visit to the castle.*

CHECKLIST
finding out what's around (4.3)
saying what you like doing (7.4)
asking if you may/can (7.7, 7.9)
asking about times and prices (4.5, 4.8, 4.9)
days of the week and expressions of time (10.2)

EXTRA PRACTICE
chapter 16 checkpoint 10

The great outdoors

Il y a un terrain de golf par ici? — *Oui, ce n'est pas loin*

Basics

où est-ce qu'on peut . . . ?		where can one/you . . . ?		
faire une promenade		to go for a walk		
faire du	ski nautique	to go	water skiing	
	canotage		boating, rowing (**un canot**, rowboat)	
	vélo		cycling	
faire de la	voile	to go	sailing	
	planche à voile		windsurfing (**une planche à voile**, sailboard)	
jouer au	tennis	to play	tennis	
	golf		golf (**des clubs de golf**, golf clubs)	
nager		to swim		
prendre un bain de soleil		to sunbathe		
louer		to hire		
location		usually tells you it's a place where you can hire things		
c'est combien	l'heure?	how much is it	an hour?	
	la journée?		a day?	
interdit		prohibited		

15.1 Finding out where to do what

Demandez à l'office de tourisme ou au syndicat d'initiative de vous indiquer où vous pouvez pratiquer votre sport préféré.

A l'office de tourisme   Imitate the holidaymaker:

TOURISTE   Où est-ce qu'on peut jouer au tennis?
HÔTESSE   Il y a des courts de tennis au Centre de Loisirs.
TOURISTE   C'est combien l'heure?
HÔTESSE   Oh ça, je ne sais pas. Il faut demander au Centre.
TOURISTE   On peut louer une raquette au Centre?
HÔTESSE   Je crois que oui.
TOURISTE   C'est ouvert tous les jours?
HÔTESSE   Oui, tous les jours, jusqu'à 19 heures.

CHECKPOINT 1   You've made your way to the **Centre de Loisirs**. How do you ask

1 where the tennis courts are
2 how much it is an hour
3 if you can hire a racket
4 if it's open on Sunday, and until what time

CHECKPOINT 2   These are the sports you're keen on.

How do you ask (a) where you can do them (b) if you can hire the necessary equipment.

CHECKPOINT 3   Everyone prefers doing different things. Listen to the cassette and fill in what they all want to do.

Ma femme préfère aller à la plage . . . . . .
Ma fille n'aime pas ça – elle veut . . . . . .
Mon fils et son ami adorent . . . . . . et . . . . . .
et moi, je voudrais . . . . . .

15.2 Understanding the brochures

When you pick up a leaflet about holiday resorts, it helps if you can recognise some of the less obvious words for the attractions they list.

baignade f.	bathing	**pêche** f.	fishing
concours m.	competition	**plongée** f. **soumarine**	skin diving
équitation f.	riding	**port** m. **de plaisance**	marina
équestre / **hippique**	equestrian	**promenade** f. **en** | **mer** / **bateau**	boat-trip
natation f.	swimming	**station** f.	resort

Read what the brochures say – guess what it all means.

Préfailles

Au coeur de la côte de Jade, avec ses belles plages et son climat doux, Préfailles vous offre ses baignades sur plages sûres et calmes, ses pêches en mer, ses courts de tennis, ses belles promenades à pied et en mer.

Pornic

Station balnéaire avec ses nombreuses plages de sable fin et criques rocheuses – golf 9 trous – courts de tennis – port de plaisance – promenades équestres – concours hippiques.

Biarritz

Vacances idéales sur la côte basque – clubs de plage – leçons de natation – activités pour les jeunes – pêche en mer et en eau douce – promenades en bateau – golf 18 trous – pêche et plongée soumarine – équitation.

CHECKPOINT 4   From the context of 15.2, what do you think these mean?

1 eau douce   3 sable fin   5 promenades à pied
2 trous   4 plages sûres   6 criques rocheuses

CHECKPOINT 5   Which of the resorts in 15.2 is most likely to appeal to

1 Arthur, a keen horseman: likes a round of golf and a game of tennis
2 Jane and Anthony: happiest in or on the water, but a long walk rates as second best
3 the Brett family: the youngest enjoy games on the beach, the older ones are crazy about skin diving, the parents enjoy a round of golf

For groups   Take it in turns to choose one of the resorts in 15.2. Say what you're going to do there – at least two things each.

For fun!   What should be on the notice boards? Choose from these:

location de canots – baignade dangereuse – pêche interdite – pique-nique interdit – canotage interdit – location de vélos

Indoor entertainments

Basics

une séance	performance, film showing
une soirée	evening entertainment
un spectacle	any kind of show
une boîte (de nuit)	nightclub
un piano bar	all-night restaurant with small band
un billet	ticket
l'entrée f., **le prix d'entrée**	admission charge
la salle	hall, auditorium, room
un bureau de location	box office (here **location** does not mean hire, see page 103)
qu'est-ce qu'il y a comme . . . ?	what sort of . . . is/are there?

15.3 **Finding out**
what's on

Consultez le journal ou demandez le programme du mois ou de la semaine
(*'What's on' brochure*) à l'office de tourisme. Si vous êtes à Paris, demandez
'Pariscope' ou 'l'Officiel des Spectacles' à un kiosque à journaux.

A l'hôtel   Imitate the tourist:

	TOURISTE	Qu'est-ce qu'on peut faire le soir?
	RÉCEPTIONNISTE	Eh bien, ça dépend. Vous aimez danser? Il y a des discothèques.
	TOURISTE	Qu'est-ce qu'il y a comme spectacles?
	RÉCEPTIONNISTE	Voilà le programme de la semaine. Mercredi soir vous pouvez assister à une soirée très intéressante.
	TOURISTE	Qu'est-ce que c'est?
	RÉCEPTIONNISTE	C'est un spectacle de variétés avec des artistes internationaux. C'est très bien, je vous assure.
	TOURISTE	Où est-ce qu'on peut acheter des billets?
	RÉCEPTIONNISTE	A la salle Picard, au bureau de location.

CHECKPOINT 6

How would you ask

1 if there are any interesting shows
2 if they have the 'What's on' brochure

3 where you can buy tickets
4 where the box office is

15.4 **Going to a**
performance

Ask for **une place** (a seat) rather than **un ticket** or **un billet**. Whether you
go to the cinema, theatre or a concert, it's the custom to give a small tip to
the usherette who also sells the programmes.

Au bureau de location   Imitate the tourist:

	TOURISTE	Vous avez des places pour mercredi soir?
	EMPLOYÉE	Je regrette, c'est complet. Mais il reste encore des places pour vendredi soir. J'ai trois places à 35F et cinq à 45F.
	TOURISTE	Alors, je prends trois places à 35F pour vendredi.
	EMPLOYÉE	Ça fait 105F, s'il vous plaît.
	TOURISTE	Le spectacle commence à quelle heure?
	EMPLOYÉE	A 20h30, et il finit vers 23h.

CHECKPOINT 7   You want to buy two tickets for the concert on Thursday evening. You don't want to spend more than 30F each. You want to know what time the concert ends. Fill in your part of the conversation.

EMPLOYÉ Vous désirez?   VOUS . . . .
         Vous voulez des places à trente francs ou à
         quarante francs?   . . . .
         Voilà! Ça vous fait soixante francs.   . . . .
         Entre 11h et 11h15.   . . . .

CHECKPOINT 8   ⊡ Listen to the cassette. What are people saying to you?

15.5 Hitting the night spots

The adverts on the entertainments pages are full of abbreviations. Days of the week are usually shortened to 3 letters: *lun = lundi* etc; *ts = tous* (every), *snc = service non compris* (service not included), *consom = consommations* (drinks), *sf = sauf* (except), *bt. = bouteille*.

These are the kinds of attractions some night spots offer:

CHEZ BOBBY, Club-discothèque, à partir de 23h. Cabaret et spectacle jeu. et ven. Topless. Ambiance. Consom. 30F. Fermé lun.

PUB MANHATTAN, Ts les soirs de 19h à 24h. Spectacles, bières anglaises.

LE SAINT, Ouvert toute la nuit. Reggae, rock moderne, pop. Entrée et consom.40F. Sam. 50F, dim. 30F. Fermé jeu.

VALENTINO, Spectacle. Specialité groupes. Chanteurs de jazz, ambiance sympathique. Ts les soirs sf dim. 22h à 6h matin. Menu à 80F & ½bt vin snc.

CHEZ JIMMY, Dîner-spectacle. Soirée inoubliable. Vieilles chansons de Paris. 20h à 24h tous les soirs sf mer. Réservation conseillée. Menu à 100F s. compris, sans surprises.

CHECKPOINT 9   When you've worked out what each night spot has to offer, say who would enjoy which one most.

Joe and Tony: pop fans looking for cheap night out to wind up holiday
Aunt Mabel: enjoys eating out and likes old-fashioned music, prefers something cosy
Mark and Paul: hard-up students on the spree, footloose on Thursday
Fred: on a barman's holiday, convinced British beer is best
Jazz club outing: motley crowd of about 25 enthusiasts

CHECKPOINT 10   ▣ Listen to the cassette and say

1 what entertainments your French friend suggests for this evening
2 what the misunderstanding is
3 what the difference is between a French pub and an English one

For groups   Let your imagination run riot. Discuss with your partner how you're going to spend the evening, choosing from the night spots in 15.5.

KEY TO CHECKPOINTS

1 1 Où sont les courts de tennis? 2 C'est combien l'heure? 3 On peut (je peux) louer une raquette? 4 C'est ouvert dimanche? Jusqu'à quelle heure?

2 (a) Où est-ce qu'on peut (je peux) jouer au tennis? . . . faire du vélo? . . . faire du canotage? . . . faire de la planche à voile? . . . jouer au golf? (b) On peut (je peux) louer une raquette? . . . un vélo (une bicyclette)? . . . un canot? . . . une planche à voile? . . . des clubs de golf?

3 prendre un bain de soleil . . . faire de la planche à voile . . . nager . . . faire du ski nautique . . . faire une petite promenade.

4 1 *fresh water*; 2 *holes*; 3 *fine sand*; 4 *safe beaches*; 5 *walks*; 6 *rocky coves*.

5 1 Pornic; 2 Préfailles; 3 Biarritz.

For fun! 1 pêche interdite; 2 baignade dangereuse; 3 pique-nique interdit; 4 canotage interdit (baignade dangereuse).

6 1 Il y a des spectacles intéressants? 2 Vous avez le programme du mois (de la semaine)? 3 Où est-ce qu'on peut (je peux) acheter des billets? 4 Où est le bureau de location?

7 VOUS: Deux places pour le concert de jeudi soir . . . A trente francs . . . Le concert finit à quelle heure?

8 1 *Sorry, we're sold out!* 2 *The admission charge is 9F.* 3 *The show starts at 8.45p.m.* 4 *Do you want tickets for the 7.30 showing?* 5 *You're going to have a very enjoyable evening!*

9 *Joe and Tony:* Le Saint; *Aunt Mabel:* Chez Jimmy; *Mark and Paul:* Chez Bobby; *Fred:* Pub Manhattan; *Jazz Club:* Valentino.

10 1 *a film, a piano bar;* 2 *thought the latter was a bar with a pianist;* 3 *A French pub is somewhere between a pub and a club, smarter and possibly more expensive than an English one. You can eat there and take the children.*

CHECKLIST
talking about yourself (6.1–6.5, 7.1–7.6)
talking about others (8.1–8.6, 9.1–9.6)
personal questions (4.4, 6.8, 7.8, 8.8)
talking about the past (10.1–10.4, 10.6)
social niceties (1.1–1.4)

EXTRA PRACTICE
chapter 6 checkpoint 14
chapter 8 checkpoint 13
chapter 9 checkpoints 10, 12
chapter 10 checkpoint 8

GETTING TO KNOW PEOPLE

Basics

vous restez combien de jours?		how many days are you staying?
vous êtes	**à quel hôtel?**	which hotel are you at?
	de quel pays?	which country are you from?
	de quelle région?	what part are you from?
	ici depuis longtemps?	have you been here long? (answer with **depuis** meaning 'for', 'since' e.g. **depuis trois jours, depuis lundi**)

16.1 **Opening gambits**

Conversation starters depend on the situation.

in the train or bus:	**vous allez loin?**	are you going far?
on the beach:	**l'eau est bonne?**	what's the water like?
in a café or train:	**cette place est libre?**	is this seat free?
anywhere:	**vous avez du feu?**	have you a light?

If all else fails, make a comment about the weather:

il fait chaud/froid/beau   it's hot/cold/lovely weather
il va pleuvoir   it's going to rain

Il va pleuvoir

Dans un café   Imitate each speaker in turn:

JEUNE HOMME   Pardon mademoiselle, cette place est libre?
JEUNE FILLE   Oui monsieur.
JEUNE HOMME   Il fait beau aujourd'hui!
JEUNE FILLE   Oui, formidable!
JEUNE HOMME   Vous êtes en vacances?
JEUNE FILLE   Oui, et vous?
JEUNE HOMME   Moi aussi. Vous connaissez la ville?
JEUNE FILLE   Non, c'est ma première visite.

CHECKPOINT 1   You're in a train and want to start talking to the couple opposite.

1 ask if they're going far   3 find out where they live
2 ask if they're on holiday   4 ask if they know England

CHECKPOINT 2   What opening gambit might start a conversation in each situation?

For groups   Using the same opening gambits, make up conversations with your partner.

16.2 **Small talk**   Asking personal questions isn't necessarily rude or inquisitive – just a way of showing interest.

Aux jardins publics   Imitate each in turn:

TOURISTE   Vous habitez ici?
FEMME   Ah non, nous sommes en vacances.
TOURISTE   Vous êtes ici depuis longtemps?
FEMME   Depuis une semaine.
TOURISTE   Vous êtes de quelle région?
FEMME   De l'Alsace. Vous connaissez l'Alsace? C'est très joli, mais il fait souvent froid.
TOURISTE   Vous êtes ici avec votre famille?
FEMME   Oui, avec mon mari et les enfants. Ils sont allés en ville pour acheter des souvenirs. Et vous, vous avez des enfants?
TOURISTE   Non, je ne suis pas mariée!
FEMME   Oh, je m'excuse!

CHECKPOINT 3   Fill in the gaps to complete the conversation on cassette.

JEUNE HOMME   L'eau est . . . ?
JEUNE FILLE   Fantastique!
JEUNE HOMME   Vous êtes bien bronzée!
JEUNE FILLE   Vous . . . ! Il fait . . . dans le Midi.
JEUNE HOMME   Ah oui, toujours. Vous êtes ici depuis . . . ?
JEUNE FILLE   Depuis . . . . . .
JEUNE HOMME   Vous . . . où?
JEUNE FILLE   A Cardiff. Vous connaissez . . . . ?
JEUNE HOMME   Mais vous êtes . . . ? Pas possible! Vous . . . pas d'accent!

CHECKPOINT 4   Listen to the cassette and say (a) what he found out about her (b) what she found out about him.

For groups   Try to find out as much as you can about each other.

Holiday chat

Basics

des projets m.pl.		plans	
faire	une excursion	to go	on an excursion
	une promenade		for a walk
passer la journée		to spend the day	
à la campagne/montagne		in or to the country/mountains	
au bord de la mer		at/to the seaside	
l'année dernière/prochaine		last/next year	

16.3 Discussing your travels

A l'hôtel, au camping, sur la plage, vous allez certainement rencontrer des Français qui seront très contents si vous parlez de vos vacances en France, de vos impressions ou de vos projets.

Au camping Imitate each holidaymaker in turn:

MME GUY Alors, Madame Brun, vous avez passé une bonne journée?

MME BRUN Très bonne, merci. Nous avons fait une belle promenade. L'après-midi nous avons visité les grottes. Les enfants adorent ça.

MME GUY Si vous aimez les grottes, il faut aller dans les Pyrénées. L'année dernière nous avons passé des vacances sensationnelles près de Pau.

MME BRUN Oh, l'année dernière, c'était un désastre pour nous! Nous sommes allés à la montagne, et il a fait très froid.

MME GUY Moi, j'adore la montagne, mais les enfants préfèrent passer les vacances au bord de la mer. Vous avez des projets pour l'année prochaine?

MME BRUN Oui, nous allons passer quinze jours au Maroc.

MME GUY Alors là, il va faire chaud, c'est sûr!

MME BRUN Et vous? Vous avez aussi des projets?

MME GUY Oui, nous voulons passer les vacances à la campagne.

Vous avez passé une bonne journée?

CHECKPOINT 5

(a) Your French friends have just returned from an outing. Ask them

1 if they had a good day
2 where they went
3 if they visited the caves
4 if it was interesting
5 if they have any plans for tomorrow
6 what they're doing this evening

(b) Now tell your friends how you spent your day. You went on an excursion to Saumur, visited the castle and the wine cellars, and bought six bottles of wine. You haven't any plans for this evening but tomorrow you're going to spend the day in the country.

Get-togethers and invitations

Basics

je vous présente . . .	may I introduce you to . . .
je vous en prie	please do!
je suis content de vous voir	I'm pleased to see you

je peux vous offrir quelque chose?	can I get you something (to drink)?
qu'est-ce que vous prenez?	what will you have (to drink)?
j'ai (un) rendez-vous	I have a date (appointment)
où est-ce qu'on se rencontre?	where shall we meet?

16.4 Social conventions

Formal invitations usually start **voulez-vous** (will you?), informal ones with **on va?** (shall we?). Accept with **avec plaisir**. More informally say **d'accord!**

If you're invited to someone's home, take flowers or a small present for your hostess. To thank her for a lovely evening say **merci pour cette soirée agréable**. More informally, say **c'était formidable!** All you need to know about shaking hands and kissing is in chapter 1 (1.3).

Au bureau du directeur Imitate each in turn:

DIRECTEUR	Bonjour Monsieur Colbert. Je suis content de vous voir. Comment allez-vous, cher ami?
M COLBERT	Très bien, merci. Et vous?
DIRECTEUR	Ça va, merci. Prenez place, je vous en prie. Je vous présente mon collègue, Gérard Duval.
M COLBERT	Enchanté, monsieur.
DIRECTEUR	Je peux vous offrir quelque chose?
M COLBERT	Merci, pas pour l'instant.
DIRECTEUR	Vous êtes libre à midi? Voulez-vous déjeuner avec nous?
M COLBERT	Avec plaisir.
DIRECTEUR	Alors comme ça, on peut parler un peu des affaires.

CHECKPOINT 6

What do you say to

1 introduce someone
2 ask someone to take a seat
3 offer someone a drink
4 invite someone to lunch (formally)
5 accept politely
6 thank your host for a lovely evening

16.5 Between friends

Close friends, relatives and young people generally use the familiar form **tu** to each other instead of **vous**.

vous comprenez?	(familiar)	tu comprends?
et vous?		et toi?
s'il vous plaît		s'il te plaît
vous avez vu votre père?		tu as vu ton père?

The **tu** form of the verb (see Language Summary) often sounds like the **je** form, e.g. **je reste**, **tu restes**. Unless you're talking to a small child, it's better to say **vous** to everyone until they suggest **alors, on se tutoie?** (let's say **tu** to each other).

A la station de ski   Imitate each in turn:

JEAN-CLAUDE	Salut Madeleine! Ça va?
MADELEINE	Salut! Ça va très bien. Et toi? Tu as fait du ski?
JEAN-CLAUDE	Bien sûr. Et toi?
MADELEINE	Moi aussi. C'était formidable!
JEAN-CLAUDE	Qu'est-ce que tu prends? Un whisky? Un diabolo-menthe?
MADELEINE	Un petit whisky, s'il te plaît . . .
JEAN-CLAUDE	(*Later.*) Qu'est-ce que tu fais ce soir? Tu restes ici? Tu veux sortir? Alors on va aller danser au Moulin Rouge?
MADELEINE	Oui, si tu veux. C'est toujours sympa!
JEAN-CLAUDE	D'accord! On va au Moulin Rouge!
MADELEINE	Où est-ce qu'on se rencontre? Au village?
JEAN-CLAUDE	Non, ici au bar, si tu préfères. C'est plus simple.
MADELEINE	D'accord! On se rencontre à quelle heure?
JEAN-CLAUDE	A huit heures et demie. Ça va?
MADELEINE	Oui – à tout à l'heure!

CHECKPOINT 7   Imagine you're having the above conversation in a more formal way. What would each of you say? Check with the cassette.

CHECKPOINT 8   How would you

1 find out where you're going to meet each other
2 say 'sorry, I have a date'
3 suggest going out this evening
4 say it was great

Keeping in touch

Basics		
quel est votre numéro de téléphone?	what's your	telephone number?
quelle est votre adresse?		address?
comment ça s'écrit?	how do you spell it?	
j'espère/nous espérons que . . .	I/we hope that . . .	
à l'année prochaine!	see you next year!	

16.6 **Exchanging details**

Make sure you can spell (19.3) and count in French. Revise numbers with the help of the page numbers and your self-checking cards (3.3).

A la salle de conférences   Imitate each in turn:

⊡	M MAUGER	Alors, vous partez demain?
	MR W-SMITH	Oui, je prends l'avion demain matin.
	M MAUGER	C'est dommage! Vous revenez en France l'année prochaine?
	MR W-SMITH	J'espère que oui.
	M MAUGER	A propos – votre nom, Willoughby-Smith, comment ça s'écrit?
	MR W-SMITH	W-I-LL-O-U-G-H-B-Y, Willoughby, S-M-I-T-H, Smith. Et voici mon adresse: 91 Montrose Way, Bristol.
	M MAUGER	Merci. Et quel est votre numéro de téléphone?
	MR W-SMITH	Bristol deux-zéro-un-six-neuf. Et quelle est votre adresse?
	M MAUGER	Voici ma carte de visite. A l'année prochaine, alors!

CHECKPOINT 9

Your friend rings you at the Hôtel de la Gare to say goodbye. Make sure she's got your home address right. It's 115 Elm Grove, York. Tel. 806034. Check with the cassette.

⊡	NINETTE	Allô! C'est Ninette à l'appareil! C'est pour vous dire au revoir.
	VOUS	*(ask when she's leaving)*
	NINETTE	Nous partons cet après-midi.
	VOUS	*(that's a pity – ask if they're coming to York next year)*
	NINETTE	Oui, j'espère.
	VOUS	*(ask if she has your address)*
	NINETTE	Oui, cent cinq Elm Grove, à York. Et votre numéro de téléphone c'est le quatre-vingts, soixante, trente-cinq, n'est-ce pas?
	VOUS	*(put her right!)*

16.7 **Writing to friends**

▶ Beginnings   The first word 'Dear . . .' will be one of these:

cher   **chère**   **chers** or    **chères**

▶ Endings

bien à vous	yours sincerely
avec mes/nos amitiés	
(bien) amicalement	best wishes, regards, yours
je vous embrasse	
nous vous embrassons	with love

▶ Special greetings

joyeux Noël!	happy Christmas!
bonne année!	happy New Year!
joyeuses Pâques!	happy Easter!
joyeux anniversaire!	happy birthday!

▶ Holiday news   This is the sort of thing you may want to write:

Chers amis, nous passons des vacances formidables sur la Côte d'Azur. Notre hôtel est très confortable, et la cuisine est excellente. Les enfants jouent sur la plage tous les jours. Hier nous avons fait une excursion à Grasse. Nous avons visité les parfumeries. C'était très intéressant. Nous espérons que vous allez bien. Avec nos amitiés . . .

CHECKPOINT 10   Write to your French friends telling them you're having a great holiday in Collioure, you're at the Hôtel Moderne etc, using the pictures as cues. (Look at the first page of chapter 15 again.)

For groups   Write holiday postcards to each other boasting about where you've been and what you did. Try to go one better than your partner.

KEY TO
CHECKPOINTS

1   1 Vous allez loin? 2 Vous êtes en vacances? 3 Vous habitez où? 4 Vous connaissez l'Angleterre?

2   1 L'eau est bonne? 2 Il va pleuvoir. 3 Cette place est libre? 4 Vous avez du feu?

3   bonne; aussi; chaud; longtemps; cinq jours; habitez; le pays de Galles; galloise; n'avez.

4   (a) *She's a non-smoker. She's staying at the Bristol Hotel for a week or two. She's on a business trip and works for an American paper.*
(b) *He's staying at the Royal Hotel, but has arranged to see some friends here in the Bristol Hotel. He's attending a conference.*

5   (a) 1 Vous avez passé une bonne journée? 2 Vous êtes allés où? 3 Vous avez visité les grottes? 4 C'était intéressant? 5 Vous avez des projets pour demain? 6 Qu'est-ce que vous faites ce soir?
(b) Nous avons fait une excursion à Saumur, nous avons visité le château et les caves, et nous avons acheté six bouteilles de vin. Nous n'avons pas de projets pour ce soir, mais demain nous allons passer la journée à la campagne.

6   1 Je vous présente . . . 2 Prenez place, je vous en prie. 3 Je peux vous offrir quelque chose? 4 Voulez-vous déjeuner avec moi (nous)? 5 Avec plaisir! 6 Merci pour cette soirée agréable. (C'était formidable!)

8   1 Où est-ce qu'on se rencontre? 2 Je regrette, j'ai (un) rendez-vous. 3 On va (Voulez-vous) sortir ce soir? 4 C'était formidable!

10   Chers amis, nous passons des vacances formidables à Collioure. Nous sommes à l'Hôtel Moderne. La cuisine est excellente (très bonne). Hier les enfants ont loué des vélos. Ils sont allés à Argèles-sur-Mer. Aujourd'hui mon mari (ma femme) et moi, nous avons fait de la voile. Nous espérons que vous allez bien. Avec nos amitiés . . .

CHECKLIST
finding your way around (4.3, 4.5, 5.2)
asking where things are (5.1)
saying what you want to do (7.6)
finding out about times (4.5)
days of the week (10.2)
understanding times, prices (4.8, 4.9) and directions (5.5)

EXTRA PRACTICE
chapter 4 checkpoint 9
chapter 20 checkpoint

Going by bus and coach

Le dernier bus part à quelle heure?

Basics

un autobus, un bus	town bus
un autocar, un car	coach, long-distance bus (never a car)
la gare routière	coach/bus station
un arrêt	stop (a request stop is **un arrêt facultatif**)
c'est quelle ligne?	which number bus is it?
un carnet	book or set of tickets (cheaper than singles)
une place	seat (also square, as in **place du Marché**)
un aller simple	single ticket
un aller-retour	return ticket
descendre	to get off
monter	to get on
le conducteur	bus driver (not conductor)
où est-ce qu'il faut . . . ?	where do you have to . . . ?

17.1 Getting the right bus

Dans la rue   Imitate the woman:

FEMME   Pardon monsieur, c'est quelle ligne pour aller au musée?
MONSIEUR   La ligne douze, madame.
FEMME   Il y a un arrêt d'autobus par ici?
MONSIEUR   Mais vous avez la gare routière à cinq cents mètres!
FEMME   C'est où, exactement?
MONSIEUR   Vous montez la rue Voltaire et vous prenez la deuxième à gauche. C'est tout de suite à droite, à côté de la mairie.

CHECKPOINT 1

1 How do you get to the bus station?
2 How far is it?
3 What number bus does the woman need?
4 Where does she want to go?

Pour aller à l'aquarium, c'est quelle ligne, s'il vous plaît?

7.2 Getting off at the right stop

Dans le bus   Imitate the tourist:

TOURISTE   Je voudrais aller à l'église du Sacré Coeur. Où est-ce qu'il faut descendre, s'il vous plaît?
CONDUCTEUR   Vous descendez rue Boileau. Vous avez un ticket?
TOURISTE   Non, je voudrais un carnet, s'il vous plaît.
CONDUCTEUR   Voilà, ça fait 25F50.
TOURISTE   S'il vous plaît, c'est où, la rue Boileau?
CONDUCTEUR   C'est l'arrêt après la place du Marché.

CHECKPOINT 2

1 Ask where the bus stop is
2 Say you want to go to the station
3 Ask which number bus goes to the station
4 Find out where you have to get off

CHECKPOINT 3

Listen to the clerk at the coach station, then fill in the missing words.

Pour Rouen il faut prendre . . .
Il y a un car toutes les . . . minutes
Vous revenez . . . . . . ?
Alors, ... - . . . ?

For groups

Team game. Using the table below, one person asks which number bus goes to a particular place. The first person to answer correctly gets a point, chooses a different place and asks which bus goes there.

ligne
20   Gare Routière – Boulevard Wilson – Musée d'Art Moderne – Mairie
24   Cinema Vox –Eglise St Jacques – Hôpital – Jardins Botaniques
82   Place du Marché – Théâtre des Jacobins – Poste – Cathédrale
84   Université – Chambre de Commerce – Piscine Municipale

Can you say it?   **Le car pour Quimper part quand?** (Practise with the cassette)

Taking the Paris métro

Basics

(see also 'Basics' for bus/coach travel on page 116)

le métro	underground
la station de métro	underground station
c'est quelle direction?	which line is it?
la sortie	exit
RER (for pronunciation see 19.3)	=**Réseau Express Régional** (fast extension of the métro to the suburbs)
un billet, un ticket	ticket
le guichet	ticket office

17.3 **Getting from A to B**

Each line is referred to by the stations at the end of the line, e.g Neuilly–Vincennes, Porte de la Chapelle–Mairie d'Issy, etc.

So to get from Champs Elysées to Tuileries, follow the signs **direction Vincennes**. For the return journey, you'll need **direction Neuilly**.

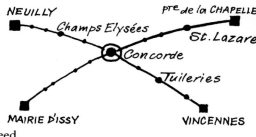

To change from one line to another, look for the sign **correspondance** (interchange), and the name of the line you need.

CHECKPOINT 4

A bewildered Englishman at Tuileries wants to go to St Lazare. He can't understand the directions he's given. Listen to the cassette and tell him in English what to do.

17.4 **Buying a métro ticket**

There's a flat rate in central Paris. You can only buy single tickets (no returns). They are also valid on Paris buses and on inner city rail services. You can get a **carnet** (a set of ten tickets) at the ticket office or from ticket machines. If you go on the **RER** you pay more and need a different or supplementary ticket.

Au guichet   Imitate the tourist:

TOURISTE	Trois aller-retour pour Concorde, s'il vous plaît.
EMPLOYÉ	Il n'y a pas de tickets aller-retour dans le métro. Vous achetez un autre ticket pour revenir.
TOURISTE	Bon, alors, trois tickets, s'il vous plaît.
EMPLOYÉ	Vous revenez par le métro?
TOURISTE	Oui, bien sûr.
EMPLOYÉ	Prenez un carnet, c'est plus avantageux.

TOURISTE   Un carnet, qu'est-ce que c'est?

EMPLOYÉ   C'est dix tickets. C'est plus ou moins le même prix que six tickets individuels.

TOURISTE   Bon, alors, un carnet s'il vous plaît.

CHECKPOINT 5   1 What was the tourist's first mistake?

2 What did the booking clerk advise him to do?

3 What saving could he make?

Going by train

Basics   (see also 'Basics' for bus/coach and métro travel on pages 116 and 118)

le bureau de renseignements	information office
la consigne	left luggage (**consigne automatique** means left luggage lockers)
en première/seconde	first/second class
le quai	platform
la voie	track (often used instead of **quai**)
un horaire	timetable
le prochain/dernier train	the next/last train
quelles sont les heures des trains pour . . . ?	what times are the trains to . . . ?
c'est direct?	is it a through train?
il faut . . .	you have to . . .
un rapide	express
un corail	air-conditioned inter-city train
un TGV ⎱ (for pronunciation	= **train à grande vitesse**, high speed train
SNCF ⎰ see 19.3)	= **Société Nationale des Chemins de Fer Français**, French Railways
le wagon-restaurant	restaurant car

Cost of drinks, snacks and meals on trains can be very high, so it's a good idea to take enough refreshments for the journey.

17.5 Getting information

French Railways in London, and British Rail can give you details of travel bargains such as **Carte Jeune** giving a 50% reduction to under-25s. In France, go to a **bureau de renseignements** for travel information.

Au bureau de renseignements   Imitate the traveller:

VOYAGEUR   Je voudrais aller à Lyon mercredi. Quelles sont les heures des trains?
EMPLOYÉ   Vous voulez partir le matin ou l'après-midi?
VOYAGEUR   Le matin.
EMPLOYÉ   Eh bien, vous avez un train à 8h13.
VOYAGEUR   C'est direct?
EMPLOYÉ   Ah non, il faut changer.
VOYAGEUR   Il y a un train direct vers 9h?
EMPLOYÉ   Non, il n'y a rien entre 8h13 et 10h. Le train de 10h est un TGV. Il faut réserver des places.
VOYAGEUR   Alors je vais prendre le TGV. Il arrive à quelle heure?
EMPLOYÉ   Il arrive à midi trente. Voici un horaire.
VOYAGEUR   Merci. On peut réserver des places ici?
EMPLOYÉ   Non, il faut aller au bureau des réservations.

CHECKPOINT 6

1 What day does he want to travel?
2 Does he want to travel in the morning, afternoon or evening?
3 Why isn't he keen on getting the 8.13?
4 What information is he given about the 10 o'clock train?
5 What else does he want to know?

17.6 Buying a train ticket

Avant de monter dans le train, compostez (*date-stamp*) votre billet. Si vous ne le faites pas, il faut payer une amende (*a fine*). Il n'est pas nécessaire de composter les billets achetés dans le Royaume Uni (*UK*).

Au guichet   Imitate the traveller:

VOYAGEUR   Paris, s'il vous plaît. Aller-retour.
EMPLOYÉ   En seconde?
VOYAGEUR   Oui. Il y a un tarif spécial pour les jeunes, n'est-ce pas?
EMPLOYÉ   Vous avez une Carte Jeune?
VOYAGEUR   Voilà!
EMPLOYÉ   Alors vous avez une réduction de cinquante pour cent. Ça fait soixante et onze francs.

VOYAGEUR   C'est à quelle heure, le prochain train?

EMPLOYÉ   Il part dans cinq minutes.

VOYAGEUR   Il part de quel quai?

EMPLOYÉ   Quai numéro quatre. N'oubliez pas de composter votre billet!

CHECKPOINT 7

1 Does he want a single or return?
2 First or second class?
3 How much does it cost?
4 Is that the normal fare?
5 When is the next train due to leave?
6 From which platform?

CHECKPOINT 8

Take the part of the traveller in this conversation.

VOUS   *(you want to go to St Tropez – ask for two singles)*

EMPLOYÉ   En première?

VOUS   *(no, second class please – ask how much)*

EMPLOYÉ   Quatre-vingt-quatre francs.

VOUS   *(ask what time the next train is)*

EMPLOYÉ   A neuf heures quinze, quai numéro treize.

VOUS   *(ask if you have to change)*

EMPLOYÉ   Non, c'est direct.

VOUS   *(find out if there's a restaurant car)*

EMPLOYÉ   Non, mais vous avez un bar.

For groups

Team game: see which team can make up the longest string of questions you might need to ask when travelling by train in France.

KEY TO CHECKPOINTS

1 1 *Go up* rue Voltaire *and take the 2nd left;* 2 *500 metres;* 3 *no.12;* 4 *the museum.*

2 1 Où est l'arrêt d'autobus? (C'est où, l'arrêt d'autobus?) 2 Je voudrais aller à la gare. 3 C'est quelle ligne pour aller à la gare? 4 Où est-ce qu'il faut descendre?

3 l'autocar; 50; ce soir; un aller-retour.

4 *You get the Neuilly line, and change at Concorde. Then you have to get the Porte de la Chapelle line and get off at St Lazare.*

5 1 *he asked for a return ticket;* 2 *to buy a carnet;* 3 *the cost of approx. four tickets.*

6 1 *Wednesday;* 2 *morning;* 3 *it's not a through train;* 4 *it's a high speed train and you have to reserve seats;* 5 *what time it arrives and if he can reserve a seat at the information office.*

7 1 *return;* 2 *second;* 3 *71F;* 4 *no, half fare;* 5 *in five minutes;* 6 *platform four.*

8 VOUS: Je voudrais aller à St Tropez. Deux allers simples . . . Non, en seconde, svp. C'est combien? . . . C'est à quelle heure, le prochain train? . . . Il faut changer? . . . Il y a un wagon-restaurant?

CHECKLIST
asking the way (5.2)
understanding directions (5.5)
asking where, when and how much (4.5, 5.1, 7.8)

EXTRA PRACTIC
chapter 20 (20.2)

Driving in France

Basics

la route	road (a route is **un itinéraire**)
la route nationale	similar to an 'A' road in Britain
l'autoroute f.	motorway
à péage	toll payable
le carrefour	crossroads
les feux m.pl. **rouges**	traffic lights (often shortened to **les feux**)
une carte	map

18.1 **Knowing the roads**

Not only do you drive on the right, at junctions you normally give way to traffic from the right (**priorité à droite**). But you have right of way on a priority road marked with a yellow-on-white sign.

During peak holiday periods, avoid bottlenecks by taking a secondary route (**itinéraire bis**) marked with a green arrow. These roads are shown on maps issued free by the French Ministry of Transport, and are available at roadside information kiosks where you see the 'clever Red Indian' character called **Bison Futé**.

Sur la route   Imitate the tourist:

TOURISTE	Pardon mademoiselle, pour aller à Rennes?
JEUNE FEMME	Vous n'avez pas de carte?
TOURISTE	Ah non, je n'ai pas de carte.
JEUNE FEMME	Bon, vous continuez tout droit jusqu'au carrefour. Là vous tournez à gauche. Quand vous arrivez à l'Auberge Impériale, vous prenez l'itinéraire bis, puis . . .
TOURISTE	Pas si vite! J'arrive à l'Auberge Impériale, et je prends l'itinéraire bis?
JEUNE FEMME	Oui, c'est ça. Puis vous continuez jusqu'à la station-service qui est sur votre gauche, et tout de suite après vous tournez à droite, et vous arrivez à la route nationale qui va directement à Rennes. Vous comprenez?
TOURISTE	Oui, oui! Merci mademoiselle. Au revoir!

CHECKPOINT 1   You ask a policeman the way from Tours to Paris. Fill in your part.

VOUS   *(ask him politely how to get to Paris)*
AGENT   Vous avez le choix entre l'autoroute et la route nationale.
        L'autoroute est plus directe, mais c'est à péage.
VOUS   *(ask if that's expensive)*
AGENT   Oui, c'est assez cher. Mais c'est beaucoup plus rapide. Si vous
        voulez prendre la route nationale, tournez à droite aux feux rouges.
VOUS   *(say you prefer the route nationale, then recap the directions)*
AGENT   C'est ça. Vous passez par Chartres et vous continuez sur la route
        nationale dix jusqu'à Paris.
VOUS   *(recap directions, then ask if it's signposted)*
AGENT   Bien sûr!

CHECKPOINT 2   Summarise in English what the policeman said, for the benefit of your
                friend who's driving.

For groups   Everyone notes down from memory words and phrases to do with
                motoring. See who makes the longest list.

Parking

Basics

on peut se garer?	is one allowed to park?
un parking	car park
gratuit/payant	free/you have to pay
libre	free (meaning spaces available)
un horodateur	'pay and display' machine
un parcmètre	parking meter
stationnement interdit défense de stationner	no parking
une amende	a fine

18.2 **Finding a place to park**   You're often allowed or even asked to park on the pavement (**le trottoir**).
Don't be misled by parking signs for **cars** – it's short for **autocars**
(coaches). Don't park in a **zone d'enlèvement** – your car will be towed
away. The same applies to a **zone piétonne** – it's a pedestrian precinct.

Dans la rue Imitate the motorist:

AUTOMOBILISTE Pardon monsieur, on peut se garer ici?

HOMME Ici? Non, non. C'est interdit. Vous risquez une amende. Je vous conseille d'aller à la gare ou au grand parking place Jobert.

AUTOMOBILISTE C'est loin, le grand parking?

HOMME Non, c'est à deux minutes.

AUTOMOBILISTE C'est gratuit?

HOMME Mais non, c'est payant. Ça vous fait trois ou quatre francs l'heure.

AUTOMOBILISTE C'est où, le parking?

HOMME Vous tournez là-bas au coin, vous montez la rue Combourg et vous prenez la petite rue à droite qui va directement au parking.

CHECKPOINT 3

1 Why can't the driver park where he is?
2 Where can he park?
3 How far away is the car park?
4 How will he get there?

CHECKPOINT 4

 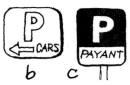 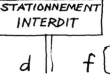 

Which signs would you park by if

1 you haven't any change
2 you want to deposit your coach load of tourists
3 you don't care where you park as long as you don't get a ticket!
4 you think you're a motorist who can always get away with it!

CHECKPOINT 5

You've arrived at your hotel and want to know where to park the car.

VOUS (*ask if they have a garage*)

RÉCEPTIONNISTE Ah non, nous n'avons pas de garage.

VOUS (*find out where one can park*)

RÉCEPTIONNISTE Il y a des parcmètres dans les petites rues près d'ici. Si vous préférez, il y a un parking au coin de la rue.

VOUS (*ask how much it is*)

RÉCEPTIONNISTE Demandez au jeune homme.

VOUS (*find out when the car park is open*)

RÉCEPTIONNISTE Jour et nuit. Pas de problème!

Going to a service station

Basics

une station-service	petrol station
de l'essence	petrol (also means 2-star petrol)
de l'ordinaire	2-star petrol
du super	4-star petrol
du gasoil	diesel
(faites) le plein	fill up the tank
voulez-vous vérifier . . . ?	would you check . . . ?
les pneus m.pl.	tyres

18.3 Getting petrol

You normally buy so many francs' worth, say 50 or 100 francs, or ask to have the tank filled up.

A la station-service   Imitate the customer:

POMPISTE	Bonjour! Vous voulez le plein?
CLIENT	Le plein? Non, pour cent francs.
POMPISTE	Du super ou de l'ordinaire?
CLIENT	Du super, s'il vous plaît. Et voulez-vous vérifier les pneus?
POMPISTE	Les pneus, bien sûr. Quelle pression?
CLIENT	Je ne sais pas. C'est une voiture de location.
POMPISTE	Je vais regarder . . . Je vérifie l'huile?
CLIENT	Merci, ce n'est pas nécessaire.
POMPISTE	C'est tout? Ça fait cent francs. Merci – et bonne route!

CHECKPOINT 6

(a) Did the driver 1 have the tank filled up 2 buy so many francs' worth of petrol 3 buy so many litres?
(b) Did the pump attendant offer to check 1 tyre pressure 2 water 3 oil?

CHECKPOINT 7

You want to fill up the tank with 4-star petrol. The only thing you want checked is the oil. You'd like to pay a call, but where are the toilets? Fill in your part.

POMPISTE	Bonjour. Vous désirez?	VOUS . . . .
	Du super ou de l'ordinaire?	. . . .
	Je vérifie les pneus?	. . . .
	Et l'eau?	. . . .
	C'est tout?	. . . .
	Il vous faut un litre. Alors, c'est tout?	. . . .
	Par ici, sur votre gauche.	

Something wrong with the car

Basics

vous pouvez m'aider?	can you help me?
je suis en panne	I've broken down
le service de dépannage	breakdown service
. . . ne marche/marchent pas	. . . isnt't/aren't working
le moteur	engine
les freins m.pl.	brakes
le pare-brise	windscreen
les phares m.pl.	headlights
j'ai un pneu à plat	I have a flat tyre
la batterie est à plat	the battery is flat
le démarreur	starter (but **le starter** is the choke!)
une pièce de rechange	spare part
à sept kilomètres de	seven kilometres from

18.4 Coping with breakdowns

Si vous êtes en panne, téléphonez à un garage et demandez le service de dépannage, ou bien téléphonez à la gendarmerie.

Sur la route nationale   Imitate the woman:

HOMME   Il ne faut pas laisser la voiture ici. C'est dangereux.
FEMME   Je sais – je suis en panne.
HOMME   Oh là là! Je peux vous aider?
FEMME   C'est très gentil. Le moteur ne marche pas.
HOMME   Les phares marchent? Oui. Alors ce n'est pas la batterie. Je ne sais pas ce que c'est. Il faut téléphoner à un garage. Vous avez de la chance. Il y a un téléphone à cent mètres d'ici.

CHECKPOINT 8

You're through to the breakdown service. Complete the conversation, then check with the cassette.

GARAGISTE   Allô, service de dépannage.
VOUS   (*ask if they can help you – say you've broken down*)
GARAGISTE   Quel est le problème?
VOUS   (*explain what the matter is*)
GARAGISTE   Vous êtes où?

VOUS   (*say you're 3 or 4 kilometres from Dijon on the* route nationale)
GARAGISTE   Qu'est-ce que vous avez comme voiture?
VOUS   (*explain that you have a small English car, and it's green*)

CHECKPOINT 9   Your car is now in a garage. Listen on cassette to the mechanic's tale of woe. What's the gist of it all?

CHECKPOINT 10   The car's giving trouble! It's a different reason every time. How would you say the headlights don't work, the engine isn't working, you have a flat tyre, the battery is flat, the windscreen is broken, and . . .

For groups   See who has the worst old banger. It's the one who can give the longest list of car faults without making a mistake!

KEY TO CHECKPOINTS

1 VOUS: Svp monsieur l'agent, pour aller à Paris . . . C'est cher? . . . Je préfère la route nationale. Je tourne à droite aux feux rouges . . . Je passe par Chartres et je continue sur la route nationale dix jusqu'à Paris. C'est indiqué?

2 *You can take the motorway or the* route nationale. *The motorway is more direct but you have to pay a toll. That's fairly expensive, but much quicker. If you want to take the* route nationale, *turn right at the lights. Go through Chartres and follow the* route nationale 10 *to Paris.*

3 1 *Because parking is prohibited.* 2 *At the station or large car park in the* place Jobert. 3 *Two minutes.* 4 *Turn down there at the corner, go up the* rue Combourg *and take the little street on the right which goes straight to the car park.*

4 1 a,e   2 b   3 a,c,e   4 b,d,f.

5 VOUS: Vous avez un garage? . . . On peut se garer où? (Où est-ce qu'on peut se garer?) . . . C'est combien? . . . Le parking est ouvert quand? (Quand est-ce que le parking est ouvert?)

6 (a) 2   (b) 3.

7 VOUS: (Faites) le plein svp . . . Du super . . . Non merci . . . Non merci . . . Voulez-vous vérifier l'huile . . . Où sont les toilettes? . . . Merci.

9 *The starter doesn't work. With English cars, it's a problem getting spares. They've phoned a big garage but are still waiting. Could you phone tomorrow around ten o'clock?*

10 Les phares ne marchent pas, le moteur ne marche pas, j'ai un pneu à plat, la batterie est à plat, le pare-brise est cassé, et les freins ne marchent pas.

Basics

téléphoner à . . .	to make a phone call to . . .
allô	hello
qui est à l'appareil?	who's speaking?
c'est de la part de qui?	who shall I say called/is calling?
on vous parle!	a call for you! you're through!
ne quittez pas!	hold the line! hold on!
raccrocher	to replace the receiver
rappeler	to call back
occupé	engaged
ça ne répond pas	no answer
un faux numéro	wrong number
faire le numéro	to dial
le correspondant	telephone subscriber
un annuaire	telephone directory
l'indicatif m.	dialling code
une cabine téléphonique	telephone box
la poste/le bureau de poste	post office
le poste	extension (e.g. **poste** 63 = extension 63)

19.1 Coping with telephone numbers

French telephone numbers include the area code and consist of figures. They are not given as a string of single digits, but like this:

96.40.60.42 **quatre-vingt-seize/quarante/soixante/quarante-deux**

46.14.37.09 **quarante-six/quatorze/trente-sept/zéro neuf**

CHECKPOINT 1   Imagine you have to give your telephone number over the phone or want to ask someone to get you a number. Practise giving these numbers, then check with the cassette.

🖭 71.21.65.75   85.92.07.46   31.50.39.41   20.87.97.16   48.12.35.20

CHECKPOINT 2   🖭 Take down the phone numbers you're given.

For groups   Everyone make up a phone number, French-style, and dictate it to the group in French. Check each one as you go.

19.2 Making and taking phone calls

Vous pouvez téléphoner depuis un bureau de poste ou une cabine téléphonique. Vous pouvez aussi téléphoner depuis un café. Le téléphone se trouve souvent à côté des toilettes.

A la poste   Imitate the tourist:

🖭   HOMME   Pardon mademoiselle, je voudrais téléphoner à Londres.
EMPLOYÉE   Allez à la cabine cinq.
HOMME   S'il vous plaît, je ne sais pas comment téléphoner à Londres.
EMPLOYÉE   Eh bien, vous faites le dix-neuf et vous attendez la tonalité.
HOMME   La tonalité. Qu'est-ce que c'est?
EMPLOYÉE   Alors la tonalité, ça fait brrrr. Puis vous faites le quarante-quatre, c'est l'indicatif pour la Grande Bretagne, puis l'indicatif local sans le premier zéro. Pour Londres, vous faites le un et non pas zéro un, et puis vous faites le numéro du correspondant.
HOMME   Merci, je vais essayer.
EMPLOYÉE   Après, vous payez ici.

CHECKPOINT 3
(a) What is the code for Britain?
(b) What number must he dial first?
(c) What is **la tonalité**?
(d) What is the code for London?

19.2 continued

A l'hôtel   Imitate the young woman phoning an acquaintance:

RÉCEPTIONNISTE   Allô – Hôtel Molière.
JEUNE FEMME   Je peux parler à Monsieur Garnier?
RÉCEPTIONNISTE   Un instant. Ne quittez pas . . . Ça ne répond pas. Vous voulez laisser un message?
JEUNE FEMME   Oui, s'il vous plaît.
RÉCEPTIONNISTE   C'est de la part de qui?
JEUNE FEMME   Madame Toussaint.
RÉCEPTIONNISTE   Voulez-vous qu'il vous rappelle?
JEUNE FEMME   Oui. Je suis à l'Hôtel Flore jusqu'à huit heures.

CHECKPOINT 4   Now try phoning a business friend. Fill in your part.

HOMME   Allô!
VOUS   *(ask who's speaking – ask if it's the Société Levêque)*
HOMME   Non, c'est un faux numéro.

(you try again – this time, you're through!)

EMPLOYÉE   Société Levêque. Bonjour.
VOUS   *(ask for Monsieur Lamballe, extension 210)*
EMPLOYÉE   C'est de la part de qui?
VOUS   *(give your name)*
EMPLOYÉE   Ne quittez pas. Le poste est occupé. Il peut vous rappeler?
VOUS   *(yes – you're at the Hôtel Impérial, room 28, until midday)*

Monsieur Gros n'est pas libre. Il peut vous rappeler?

CHECKPOINT 5   Your turn to take a phone call. Check with the cassette.

VOUS   *(phone rings – what do you say when you answer it?)*
MLLE FOURNIER   Je peux parler à Jacques, s'il vous plaît?
VOUS   *(say he has gone out – ask who's speaking)*
MLLE FOURNIER   C'est Mademoiselle Fournier. Il revient à quelle heure?
VOUS   *(you don't know – ask if she wants to leave a message)*
MLLE FOURNIER   Non, non. Je vais le rappeler vers neuf heures.
VOUS   *(say O.K., then say goodbye to her)*

CHECKPOINT 6   What is the person at the other end of the line telling you?

For groups   Practise ringing each other up and asking if you can speak to so-and-so, leaving messages etc.

19.3 Spelling it out

You may need to spell out details over the phone. This is what the alphabet sounds like – imitate what you hear.

A **â** *as in* **pâté**
B **bé**
C **cé**
D **dé**
E **e** *as in* **le**
F *similar to English*
G **gé** *as in* **mangé**
H **ach** *as in* **acheté**
I **i** *as in* **dix**

J **gi** *as in* **Gigi**
K **kha** *as in* **khaki**
L
M *similar to English*
N
O
P **pé**
Q **ku** *to rhyme with* **du**
R **aire** *as in* **faire**

S *similar to English*
T **té**
U **u** *as in* **du**
V **vé**
W *pronounced* 'doo-bleuh-vay'
X *pronounced* 'eeks'
Y *pronounced* 'eegrek'
Z *similar to English*

LL *is* **deux ell**, **TT** *is* **deux té** etc.

Practise spelling your name and address.

CHECKPOINT 7

Spell these names, then check with the cassette.

Jones Bratt Quick White Veyzey Paxman Fielding Ross

For groups

Choose a name, spell it in French and get your partner to write it down. For a bit of variety, try playing h a n g m a n in French!

For fun!

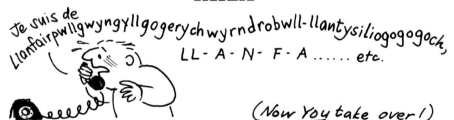

Je suis de Llanfairpwllgwyngyllgogerychwyrndrobwll-llantysiliogogogoch,
LL - A - N - F - A ...... etc.

(Now YOU take over!)

KEY TO CHECKPOINTS

2 (a) 65.23.56.08 (b) 37.93.72.18 (c) 98.32.27.15 (d) 49.70.71.10 (e) 54.44.14.41, 54.44.15.51.

3 (a) 44 (b) 19 (c) tone after dialling 19 (d) 1.

4 VOUS: Qui est à l'appareil? C'est la Société Levêque? . . . Monsieur Lamballe, svp, poste deux cent dix . . . (*give your name*) . . . Oui, je suis à l'Hôtel Impérial, chambre vingt-huit, jusqu'à midi.

6 *hold on; a call for you; replace the receiver; you have a wrong number; who's speaking?; call back this afternoon; the number is engaged.*

CHECKLIST

saying what you want to do (7.6)
asking if you may/can (7.7, 7.9)
asking where and how much (4.5, 5.1)
'some' and 'any' (2.8, 2.7, 6.5)
saying at what price (3.4)
numbers (2.2, 3.3, 4.7, 5.4, 6.6)

EXTRA PRACTICE

chapter 11 (11.5)
chapter 15 (15.4) & checkpoint 7

Basics	la monnaie	small change (rarely money, that's **argent** m.)
	un billet	bank note (there are 20F, 50F, 100F, 200F and 500F notes)
	une pièce	coin (there are 5c, 10c, 20c, 50c, 1F, 2F, 5F and 10F coins)
	une pièce d'identité	means of identification
	la livre	pound (the English pound is **la livre sterling**)
	le cours (du change)	rate of exchange (to find out about it, ask **quel est le cours de la livre/du dollar** etc?)
	un chèque de voyage	traveller's cheque (usually called **un traveller**)
	la caisse	cash desk, checkout, cashier's (in bank). **Caisse d'Epargne** is a Savings Bank
	l'addition f.	bill (for meals, drinks etc)
	la note	hotel bill
	régler	to settle (bill)
	un reçu	receipt (but a till receipt is **un ticket**)
	ça fait . . .	it comes to . . .
	où est-ce qu'on peut . . . ?	where can you/one . . . ?
	un changeur de monnaie	coin-changing machine

20.1 **Changing money**

Banks usually open Mondays–Fridays, mornings and afternoons, but close over lunch. In small towns they often open Tuesdays–Saturdays. The names of some start with **Crédit** or **Société**, e.g. **Crédit Agricole, Société Générale**. If you don't want to go to a bank, you can change currency and travellers' cheques at a **Caisse d'Epargne**.

A la banque   Imitate the tourist:

TOURISTE   Bonjour. Où est-ce qu'on peut changer des livres?

EMPLOYÉ   C'est ici, monsieur. Des livres sterling? Des billets ou des travellers?

TOURISTE   Des travellers. Quel est le cours de la livre sterling?

EMPLOYÉ   Attendez . . . Onze francs quatre-vingt-huit. Combien de livres voulez-vous changer?

TOURISTE   Trente livres. Voilà mon passeport!

EMPLOYÉ   Merci, ce n'est pas nécessaire . . . Voilà votre argent, monsieur!

CHECKPOINT 1

Cover up the conversation and fill in the missing words from memory.

1 Où est-ce qu'on peut changer des . . . ?

2 Quel est le . . . de la livre . . . ?

3 Voilà votre . . . !

4 Combien de livres voulez-vous . . . ?

CHECKPOINT 2

Take part in this conversation in a bank. Then check with the cassette.

VOUS   *(ask where you can change traveller's cheques)*

EMPLOYÉ   Des chèques de voyage? C'est ici. Vous voulez changer des dollars?

VOUS   *(no, English pounds – find out the rate of exchange)*

EMPLOYÉ   Aujourd'hui le cours de la livre sterling est de onze francs soixante-dix. Vous voulez changer combien?

VOUS   *(you'd like to change £100)*

EMPLOYÉ   Vous avez une pièce d'identité?

VOUS   *(say something as you give him your passport)*

EMPLOYÉ   Merci. Signez les chèques ici, s'il vous plaît. Passez à la caisse numéro deux.

VOUS   *(ask where it is)*

EMPLOYÉ   Là! Juste à côté.

20.2 **Getting small change**

Pardon monsieur l'agent, vous avez de la monnaie pour le parcmètre, s'il vous plaît?

There are many automatic machines about for stamps, tickets, parking fees etc which will gobble up all your small change. On many it says **faites** (or **faire) l'appoint** (put in exact money), or **l'appareil ne rend pas la monnaie** (no change given).

Dans la rue   Imitate the tourist who needs change for a parking meter:

AUTOMOBILISTE	Pardon monsieur, vous pouvez changer vingt francs?
HOMME	Qu'est-ce qu'il vous faut, madame, comme monnaie?
AUTOMOBILISTE	Des pièces de un franc. C'est pour le parcmètre.
HOMME	J'ai cinq pièces de un franc. Ça vous va?
AUTOMOBILISTE	Oui, très bien.
HOMME	Alors un, deux, trois, quatre, cinq francs. Et cinq francs, et dix!
AUTOMOBILISTE	Merci beaucoup.
HOMME	De rien!

CHECKPOINT 3

You need a metro ticket, but haven't the right change for the machine. Fill in your part of the conversation.

VOUS	*(ask a man politely if he has any small change)*
MONSIEUR	Non, je n'ai pas de monnaie.
VOUS	*(ask a young girl if she can change 10F)*
JEUNE FILLE	Je regrette . . .
VOUS	*(find out from the next person where you can change 10F coins)*
HOMME	Mais, dans un changeur de monnaie!
VOUS	*(ask what that is)*
HOMME	Mais . . . c'est une machine pour changer la monnaie. C'est un changeur automatique.
VOUS	*(ask if there's a coin-changing machine around)*

CHECKPOINT 4

Test your memory. These words are not what they look like – say what they mean. Check with 'Basics' on page 132.

pièce   billet   monnaie   travellers   note   cours   addition   ticket

20.3 Paying the hotel bill

On your hotel bill you'll often see **TTC** (**toutes taxes comprises**), meaning inclusive of tax. **TVA** (**taxe à la valeur ajoutée**) means VAT.

A la réception   Imitate the hotel guest:

CLIENT	La note, s'il vous plaît.
PATRONNE	Oui, c'est quelle chambre?
CLIENT	Vingt-sept.
PATRONNE	Un instant, s'il vous plaît. Vous partez tout de suite?
CLIENT	Oui, je prends le train de dix heures.
PATRONNE	Vous voulez régler comment?
CLIENT	Vous acceptez les cartes de crédit?
PATRONNE	Bien sûr! Voilà votre note.
CLIENT	Merci. Pardon madame, il y a une petite erreur. Qu'est-ce que c'est, déjeuner, cinquante-six francs?
PATRONNE	Vous n'avez pas pris le déjeuner le jour de votre arrivée?
CLIENT	Non, je suis arrivé le soir.
PATRONNE	Je m'excuse. C'est exact. Vous êtes arrivé le soir. Alors ça fait six cent quarante-deux francs moins cinquante-six francs . . . Cinq cent quatre-vingt-six francs.
CLIENT	C'est avec service et taxes?
PATRONNE	Oui, taxes et service sont compris.

CHECKPOINT 5

1 How does the hotel guest pay the bill?
2 Is it correct?
3 Is the final total 642F, 656F or 586F?
4 Is it inclusive of tax and service?
5 Did he arrive before or after lunch on his first day?

For groups

Hold your own auction! Assume each student has 100F with which to bid. Try to buy as many items as possible without overspending. Appoint an auctioneer who writes up the name of the article to be auctioned, e.g. **une bouteille de vin**, **un chapeau**, and starts bidding at a low price. Students keep bidding until no one is prepared to go any higher. Highest bidder makes a note of what he has bought and the price paid, and the auctioneer continues with the next item.

KEY TO CHECKPOINTS

1   1 livres; 2 cours, sterling; 3 argent; 4 changer.
2   VOUS: Où est-ce qu'on peut (je peux) changer des travellers? . . . Non, des livres sterling . . . Quel est le cours? . . . Je voudrais changer cent livres . . . Voilà mon passeport! . . . C'est où?
3   VOUS: Pardon monsieur, vous avez de la monnaie svp? . . . Pardon mademoiselle, vous pouvez changer dix francs? . . . Où est-ce qu'on peut (je peux) changer des pièces de dix francs? . . . Qu'est-ce que c'est? . . . Il y a un changeur de monnaie par ici?
5   1 *by credit card*; 2 *no*; 3 *586F*; 4 *yes*; 5 *after lunch*.

CHECKLIST
saying what has happened (10.1, 10.3, 10.4)
saying when (10.2)
describing things (3.1, 6.2, 8.7, 9.7)
asking for things (2.5–2.7)
saying what someone has or hasn't got (6.5, 8.4)

EXTRA PRACTICE
chapter 18 checkpoints 8, 9 & 1(
also 18.4

In a fix

Basics

vous pouvez m'aider?	can you help me?
vous pouvez réparer . . . ?	can you mend . . . ?
j'ai cassé . . .	I've broken . . .
je ne peux pas	I can't (but 'I can't find' is **je ne trouve pas**)
. . . ne marche(nt) pas	. . . doesn't/don't work
une épingle de sûreté	safety pin
une fermeture éclair	zip fastener
du scotch	some sellotape (also means 'whisky')
un tire-bouchon	corkscrew
un ouvre-boîtes	tin opener

21.1 Coping with snags

People will usually help in a big emergency without being asked. It's the minor mishaps which may not be so obvious until you say something.

Vous avez une épingle de sûreté?

CHECKPOINT 1

Work out which phrase from the selection on the right you would need in each of the situations 1–6.

1 You've broken your glasses
2 You can't close the door of your room
3 A vital zip fastener refuses to stay done up
4 You've torn your map of France
5 No sign of your corkscrew
6 You've split your best trousers

a **Vous avez une épingle de sûreté?**
b **Vous pouvez réparer mon pantalon?**
c **Je ne peux pas fermer la porte de ma chambre**
d **Je ne trouve pas le tire-bouchon**
e **Vous avez du scotch?**
f **J'ai cassé mes lunettes**

CHECKPOINT 2   How would you deal with these situations? Check with the cassette.

1 Tell the woman waiting for the lift that it doesn't work
2 Ask the optician if he can mend your glasses
3 Tell the car park attendant you can't find your car. Ask if he can help you
4 Nothing to open the baked beans with! Ask your fellow-campers if they have a tin opener
5 Ring reception for help – you can't open the door of your room

Lost something?

Basics

| **j'ai perdu/laissé/oublié** | I've lost/left behind/forgotten |
| | |

en | **cuir/plastique** | made of | leather/plastic
or/argent | | gold/silver (**argent** is also money)

rouge	red	**noir**	black
bleu	blue	**gris**	grey
vert	green	**blanc**	white (fem. form is **blanche**)
jaune	yellow	**marron**	brown (never changes)

21.2 Giving particulars

Si vous avez perdu quelque chose, allez au bureau des objets trouvés (*lost property office*), ou bien à la gendarmerie ou au commissariat de police (*police station*). Et bonne chance!

Au commissariat   Imitate the woman:

AGENT   Je peux vous aider?
FEMME   J'ai perdu mon sac à main.
AGENT   Vous l'avez laissé où?
FEMME   Dans une cabine téléphonique, en face de l'hôtel de ville.
AGENT   Vous l'avez perdu quand?
FEMME   Ce matin, vers midi.
AGENT   Il est comment, votre sac?
FEMME   Il est en cuir noir, pas très grand. Comme ça!
AGENT   Qu'est-ce qu'il contenait?
FEMME   Un peu d'argent, pas beaucoup – cinquante francs peut-être – mes clés et une photo de mes enfants.
AGENT   Un petit instant madame, je vais voir.

CHECKPOINT 3   1 Where did she leave her handbag?   3 What is it like?
                              2 When did she lose it?   4 What is in it?

CHECKPOINT 4   Say who has left what where, and describe it.

person	item	where left	description
1 you	hat	beach	grey
2 your father	suitcase	train	white, plastic
3 your sister	handbag	dining room	brown, leather
4 friend (male)	lighter	taxi	silver
5 friend (female)	bracelet	room	gold, very old

For groups   Each describe something you've lost. The others must guess what it is.

Minor ailments

Basics

un médecin	doctor
un médicament	medicine (see also 'Sidelines' on page 45)
un comprimé	tablet
une angine	throat infection (not angina)
je suis malade	I'm ill
j'ai la grippe	I've got 'flu (not stomach pains)
j'ai de la fièvre	I have a temperature

	à la tête/gorge	I've a headache/sore throat
j'ai mal	**à l'estomac**	I've a stomach ache
	aux dents	I've a toothache
	au coeur	I feel sick (although **coeur** means heart, there's no connection here)

Nous avons mal à la tête, chéri

21.3 **Going to the chemist's**   A chemist can often suggest treatment for minor ailments and mishaps. This may be in the form of suppositories (**des suppositoires**), not tablets. Thermometers may also go the way of suppositories, especially when doctors attend small children.

A la pharmacie   Imitate the customer:

MONSIEUR   S'il vous plaît, ma femme est malade. Elle a mal à l'estomac. Qu'est-ce que vous avez comme médicament?

PHARMACIEN   Ça dépend. Elle a de la fièvre?

MONSIEUR   Non, non, elle n'a pas de fièvre.

PHARMACIEN   Elle a mal au coeur?

MONSIEUR   Oui, un peu. Nous avons mangé des huîtres hier soir.

PHARMACIEN   C'est peut-être ça. Je vais vous donner quelque chose. Vous préférez des suppositoires ou des comprimés?

MONSIEUR   Des comprimés, s'il vous plaît.

PHARMACIEN   Bon alors, il faut prendre deux comprimés toutes les deux heures.

CHECKPOINT 5   How do you explain that you have a sore throat, you don't have a temperature, you'd like some tablets, you don't like suppositories.

CHECKPOINT 6   Say what's the matter with each one:

For groups   Imagine you're in a doctor's waiting room telling each other what's the matter with you.

KEY TO
CHECKPOINTS
1   1 f   2 c   3 a   4 e   5 d   6 b
3   1 *In a phone box opposite the town hall. 2 This morning about midday.*
3 Black leather, not very big. 4 About 50F, keys and a photo of her children.
4   1 J'ai laissé mon chapeau sur la plage. Il est gris.   2 Mon père a laissé sa valise dans le train. Elle est blanche. Elle est en plastique.   3 Ma soeur a laissé son sac à main dans la salle à manger. Il est marron. Il est en cuir. 4 Mon ami a laissé son briquet dans le taxi. Il est en argent.   5 Mon amie a laissé son bracelet dans sa chambre. Il est en or. Il est très vieux.
5   J'ai mal à la gorge, je n'ai pas de fièvre, je voudrais des comprimés, je n'aime pas les suppositoires.
6   1 Il a mal à la tête. 2 Elle a mal aux pieds. 3 Il a mal au coeur. 4 Elle a mal aux dents. 5 Il est malade (Il a de la fièvre).

Can you say it   **cuir gris**   (See how many times you can say that in quick succession without laughing – or choking!)

The Language Summary deals with the main points introduced in the course.

	singular			plural
	with masc. nouns	with fem. nouns	with m. & f. nouns starting with vowel and often **h**	
a/an	**un**	**une**	**un** m. **une** f.	
the	**le**	**la**	**l'**	**les**
to the, at the, in the, on the	**au**	**à la**	**à l'**	**aux**
some, any, of the, from the	**du**	**de la**	**de l'**	**des**
my	**mon**	**ma**	**mon**	**mes**
his	**son**	**sa**	**son**	**ses**
her	**son**	**sa**	**son**	**ses**
our	**notre**	**notre**	**notre**	**nos**
your	**votre**	**votre**	**votre**	**vos**
your (familiar)	**ton**	**ta**	**ton**	**tes**
their	**leur**	**leur**	**leur**	**leurs**
this	**ce**	**cette**	**cet** m. **cette** f.	**ces**
which	**quel**	**quelle**	**quel** m. **quelle** f.	**quels** m. **quelles** f.

Plural of nouns

	singular	plural
Most add **-s**	**le train**	**les trains**
	la voiture	**les voitures**
No change when they end in **-s** or **-x**	**le bus**	**les bus**
	le prix	**les prix**
Those ending in **-au** and **-eu** usually add **-x**	**le château**	**les châteaux**
	le feu	**les feux**
Most ending in **-al** change to **-aux**	**le journal**	**les journaux**

Adjectives

▶ These very common adjectives come before the noun:

beau   bon   grand   jeune   joli   petit   vieux
e.g.   **un grand hôtel   une jeune femme**

▶ Others come after:

e.g.   **un hôtel confortable   une femme charmante**

▶ Whatever their position, most adjectives change their endings when describing fem. or plural nouns. (See next page.)

Adjectives continued

	masc. sing.	fem. sing. add **-e** but not to those already ending in **-e**	masc. plural add **-s** but not to those already ending in **-s** or **-x**	fem. plural add **-s** to the fem. sing.
basic pattern	**anglais** **grand** **jeune**	**anglaise** **grande** **jeune**	**anglais** **grands** **jeunes**	**anglaises** **grandes** **jeunes**
variations adj. ending in **-er**	**dernier**	change to **-ère** **dernière**	**derniers**	**dernières**
-al	**national**	**nationale**	change to **-aux** **nationaux**	**nationales**
-el **-il** **-ien** **-on**	**sensationnel** **gentil** **indien** **bon**	double **l** or **n** **sensationnelle** **gentille** **indienne** **bonne**	**sensationnels** **gentils** **indiens** **bons**	**sensationnelles** **gentilles** **indiennes** **bonnes**
-eux **-oux**	**affreux** **jaloux**	change **-x** to **-se** **affreuse** **jalouse**	**affreux** **jaloux**	**affreuses** **jalouses**
odd ones out	**blanc** **doux** **marron** **beau (bel★)** **vieux (vieil★)**	**blanche** **douce** **marron** **belle** **vieille**	**blancs** **doux** **marron** **beaux** **vieux**	**blanches** **douces** **marron** **belles** **vieilles**

★ before a vowel and often **h**

Present

Verbs ending in '-er'

	basic pattern	variations		odd one out
		accent changes	**l** changes to **ll**	
	parler (to speak)	**préférer** (to prefer)	**rappeler** (to call back)	**aller** (to go)
je	**parle**	**préfère**	**rappelle**	**vais**
tu	**parles**	**préfères**	**rappelles**	**vas**
il/elle/on	**parle**	**préfère**	**rappelle**	**va**
nous	**parlons**	**préférons**	**rappelons**	**allons**
vous	**parlez**	**préférez**	**rappelez**	**allez**
ils/elles	**parlent**	**préfèrent**	**rappellent**	**vont**

▶ **espérer** (to hope) is like **préférer**; **s'appeler** (to be called) is like **rappeler**
▶ **il/elle** and **ils/elles** refer to things as well as people
▶ **on** means one, you, people, we (in a general sense)
▶ **je parle** etc can mean I speak or I am speaking etc. The same applies to many other verbs

Verbs ending in '-re', '-ir', '-oir'

Their pattern varies. They are given here in alphabetical order.

	attendre to wait (for)	avoir to have	comprendre to understand	connaître to know
je (j')	attends	ai	comprends	connais
tu	attends	as	comprends	connais
il/elle/on	attend	a	comprend	connaît
nous	attendons	avons	comprenons	connaissons
vous	attendez	avez	comprenez	connaissez
ils/elles	attendent	ont	comprennent	connaissent

	descendre to go/come down	être to be	faire to do/make	finir to finish
je	descends	suis	fais	finis
tu	descends	es	fais	finis
il/elle/on	descend	est	fait	finit
nous	descendons	sommes	faisons	finissons
vous	descendez	êtes	faites	finissez
ils/elles	descendent	sont	font	finissent

	ouvrir to open	partir to leave	pouvoir to be able (to)	prendre to take
je (j')	ouvre	pars	peux	prends
tu	ouvres	pars	peux	prends
il/elle/on	ouvre	part	peut	prend
nous	ouvrons	partons	pouvons	prenons
vous	ouvrez	partez	pouvez	prenez
ils/elles	ouvrent	partent	peuvent	prennent

	revenir to come back	sortir to come/go out	venir to come	vouloir to want (to)
je	reviens	sors	viens	veux
tu	reviens	sors	viens	veux
il/elle/on	revient	sort	vient	veut
nous	revenons	sortons	venons	voulons
vous	revenez	sortez	venez	voulez
ils/elles	reviennent	sortent	viennent	veulent

Past

You form the perfect tense with the present of **avoir** (in some cases **être** 10.4) and the past participle.

Verbs ending in '-er'

All past participles end in -é.
parler   j'ai parlé etc   **aller   je suis allé(e)** etc

Verbs ending in '-re', '-ir', '-oir'

Most past participles end in **-u**, **-i**, **-is** or **-t**.

comprendre	j'ai compris etc	perdre	j'ai perdu etc
écrire	j'ai écrit	prendre	j'ai pris
faire	j'ai fait	recevoir	j'ai reçu
finir	j'ai fini	sortir	je suis sorti(e)
partir	je suis parti(e)	voir	j'ai vu

▶ With verbs suggesting coming, going, staying, you use the present of **être** and the past participle which then changes like an adjective e.g. **Ma femme est allée au marché. Nos amis sont partis hier.**

▶ **J'ai parlé** etc can mean I spoke or I have spoken etc; **il est parti** etc can mean he left or he has left. The same applies to many other verbs.

Ways of asking questions

Colloquial

Turn a statement into a question by raising your voice at the end. The answer is usually yes or no.

Vous aimez la France?   C'est votre valise?
Il y a des excursions?   Elle va bien?

To ask where, when, how etc add a question word at the end.

Vous habitez où?   Il s'appelle comment?   Le bus arrive quand?

Less colloquial

Start with **est-ce que** (it has no equivalent in English) and continue with a statement.

Est-ce que vous aimez la France?   Est-ce que c'est votre valise?
Est-ce qu'il y a des excursions?   Est-ce qu'elle va bien?

To ask where, when, how etc put the question word before **est-ce que**.

Où est-ce que vous habitez?
Comment est-ce qu'il s'appelle?
Quand est-ce que le bus arrive?

More formal

Change the word order.

Aimez-vous la France?
Où habitez-vous?
Comment s'appelle-t-il?

To make a smooth liaison always pronounce **d★** and **t** before **il(s)** and **elle(s)**. If there isn't a **t** there, add one.

Comment s'appellent-ils?   Comprend★-elle le français?
Comment s'appelle-t-il?   Va-t-elle bien?

★ **d** is pronounced like **t**

This gives you the French and English words you need for working through the course. The translations apply to the context in which the words appear. Words where the meaning is obvious are omitted.

The past participles of verbs other than those ending in **-er**, which all end in **-é**, are given in brackets. An asterisk means that they are used with **être**. The fem. ending of adjectives is shown in brackets. Reference numbers tell you the section or page to consult for more details.

a *has*
à *in, to* (5.2, 9.1), *at, for, on*
a(n) un, une
d'accord *OK, all right*
acheter *to buy*
l'addition f. *bill (for meal)*
address l'adresse f.
admission charge l'entrée f.
to adore adorer
les affaires f.pl. *business*
afternoon l'après-midi m.
after-shave l'après-rasage m.
l'agent m. *policeman*
j'ai *I have*
aimer *to like, love*
airport l'aéroport m.
aller★ *to go* (p 141, 10.3);
  (*see also* 1.3, 8.8, 9.2)
l'aller-retour m. *return ticket*
l'aller m. simple *single ticket*
allô *hello (on phone)*
alors *well then, so*
I am je suis
I am . . . years old j'ai . . . ans
  (6.7)
l'amende f. *fine*
American américain(-e)
l'ami m. *friend, boyfriend*
l'amie f. *girlfriend*
l'an m. *year*
and et
anglais(-e) *English, British*
l'Anglais m. *Englishman*
l'Angleterre f. *England*
l'année f. *year*
any du, de l', de la, des,
  de, d'
anything cheaper moins cher
l'appareil m. *machine; telephone*
à l'appareil *speaking (on phone)*
l'appartement m. *flat*
s'appeler *to be called* (p 141)
apporter *to bring*

après *then, after, afterwards*
l'après-midi m. *(in the) afternoon*
l'après-rasage m. *after-shave*
are sommes, êtes, sont
  (*from* être p 142)
l'argent m. *money, silver*
around par ici
l'arrêt m. *stop*
to arrive arriver★ (10.4)
l'arrivée f. *arrival*
tu as *you have (familiar)* (16.5)
l'ascenseur m. *lift*
assez *rather*
assister à *to attend, go to*
at à
at home à la maison
attendre (attendu) *to wait*
  (*for*) (p 142)
au(x) *to the* (5.2), *on the, at*
  the, in the
l'auberge f. *inn*
aujourd'hui *today*
aussi *too, also*
l'autocar m. *long-distance bus,*
  coach
l'autoroute f. *motorway*
autre *other*
autre chose *anything else*
à l'avance *beforehand*
avant de *before*
avantageux(-se) *favourable*
avec *with*
avez: vous avez *you have*
l'avion m. *plane*
avoir *to have* (p 142)
avons: nous avons *we have*
awful affreux(-se)

baby le bébé
la baignade *bathing*
le bain *bath*
  prendre un bain de
  soleil *to sunbathe*

baker's la boulangerie
balnéaire: la station
  balnéaire *seaside/health*
  resort
la banque *bank*
bar le bar
le bateau *boat*
battery la batterie
beach la plage
beau (f. belle) *beautiful,*
  good-looking (8.5)
beaucoup *much, a lot*
beautiful beau (f. belle)
les beaux-arts m.pl. *fine arts*
beer la bière
bel (f. belle) *beautiful, good-*
  looking (8.5)
le beurre *butter*
bicycle le vélo, la bicyclette
la bière *beer*
bien *well, fine, nice*
bien sûr *of course, sure*
big grand(-e)
bill (for meal) l'addition f.
le billet *ticket, (bank)note*
black noir(-e)
blanc (f. blanche) *white*
blanket la couverture
bleu(-e) *blue; rare (meat)*
le bloc sanitaire *washing*
  facilities
la boisson *drink*
la boîte (aux lettres) *(letter)box*
le bol *bowl*
bon *OK, I see*
bon(-ne) *good*
bonjour *good morning/*
  afternoon, hello
bonsoir *good evening, hello*
to book réserver
bookshop la librairie
au bord de la mer *at the*
  seaside, by the sea

boss le patron
bottle la bouteille
la boulangerie *baker's*
la bouteille *bottle*
box office le bureau de location
boyfriend l'ami m.
bracelet le bracelet
la brasserie *eating-place* (13.1)
bread le pain
breakfast le petit déjeuner
la Bretagne *Brittany*
bridge le pont
Brittany la Bretagne
broken cassé(-e)
broken down en panne
bronzé(-e) *suntanned*
brother le frère
brown marron (*never changes*)
brûlé(-e) *burnt*
le bureau *office*
le bureau de location *box office*
le bureau de renseignements
    information office
le bureau des réservations
    booking office
bus le bus, l'autobus m.
bus stop l'arrêt m. d'autobus
businessman l'homme m.
    d'affaires
business trip le voyage d'affaires
but mais
butcher's la boucherie; la
    charcuterie (*for pork meats*)
butter le beurre
to buy acheter

c = centime(s)
c' = ce
ça *that, it*
la cabine téléphonique *phone
    box*
le cabinet de toilette *basin and
    bidet*
le café *coffee, café*
la caisse *cash desk, cashier's,
    ticket office*
cake shop la pâtisserie
la campagne *country(side)*
le camping *campsite, camping*

can I/one je peux, on peut
    (7.7, 7.9)
Canadian canadien(-ne)
le canot *rowboat*
le canotage: faire du canotage
    to go rowing
le car (*short for* autocar) *coach,
    long-distance bus*
car la voiture
    to go by car être en voiture
car park le parking
le carrefour *crossroads*
la carte *menu; map; card*
le casino *casino*
cassé *broken*
castle le château
cat le chat
to catch (*train etc*) prendre (p 142)
cathedral la cathédrale
la cave *wine cellar*
cave la grotte
ce *that, it; this* (10.2)
ce que *what*
cent *hundred*
la cerise *cherry*
cet(-te) *this, that* (10.2)
la chambre (*bed*)*room*
la chance *luck*
change (*small*) la monnaie
to change changer
le changeur de monnaie *coin-
    changing machine*
la chanson *song*
le chanteur *singer*
le chapeau *hat*
le chapitre *chapter*
chaque *every, each*
charming charmant(-e)
le chat *cat*
le château *castle, palace*
chaud(-e) *warm, hot*
le chauffage *heating*
chauffé(e) *heated*
to check vérifier
cheese le fromage
le chef-d'oeuvre *masterpiece*
chemist's la pharmacie
cher(-ère) *expensive; dear*
chercher *to look for*

chéri m., chérie f. *darling*
le chèvre *goat's cheese*
chez *at* (*someone's place*)
le chien *dog*
children les enfants m.pl.
choisi *chosen, decided*
le choix *choice*
church l'église f.
cigarette la cigarette
cinema le cinéma
cinq *five*
cinquante *fifty*
cinquième *fifth*
class (*2nd*) en deuxième
la clé *key* (*also spelt* clef)
to close fermer
coach l'autocar m., le car
le cochon *pig*
le coeur *heart*
coffee le café
le cognac *brandy*
le coiffeur *hairdresser*
la coiffeuse (*woman*) *hairdresser*
au coin *on the corner*
coin la pièce
coin-changing machine le
    changeur de monnaie
colleague le collègue
combien (de) *how much/many*
to come venir* (p 142, 10.4)
comfortable confortable
commander *to order*
comme *as, like, by way of*
comment *how, how to, what*
comment est . . . ? *what
    is . . . like?*
le commissariat (de police)
    police station
complet(-ète) *full, fully
    booked, sold out*
composter *to date-stamp*
comprendre (compris) *to
    understand* (p 142)
le comprimé *tablet*
compris *included; understood*
concert le concert
connaître (connu) *to know*
    (*people, places*) (p 142)
conseiller *to advise*

to consult consulter
contenait *contained*
content(-e) (de) *happy,*
    pleased (to)
cooking la cuisine
le correspondant *subscriber*
la côte *coast*
à côté *next door*
à côté de *next to*
cotton en coton
country le pays
la cour *court*
le cours (du change)
    (exchange) rate
les courses f.pl. *shopping*
coûter *to cost*
la crêperie *pancake house*
les crevettes f.pl. *shrimps, prawns*
je crois (que oui) *I think (so)*
le cuir *leather*
la cuisine *cooking, food; kitchen*
cuit: bien cuit *well done(meat)*
cup la tasse
cycling: to go cycling faire du
    vélo

d' = de
to dance danser
dangereux(-se) *dangerous*
dans *in*
date: I've a date j'ai (un)
    rendez-vous
daughter la fille
day le jour, la journée
de (d') *of, to, from, about;*
    some, any (2.8, 2.7)
de l', de la *of the, to the;*
    some, any (2.8, 2.7)
défense de *prohibited*
la dégustation *tasting*
déjeuner *to have lunch*
le déjeuner *lunch*
    le petit déjeuner *breakfast*
demain *tomorrow*
à demain *see you tomorrow*
demander *to ask (for)*
demi- . . . *half (a)*
et demie *half past*
la dent *tooth*

le dépannage: le service de
    dépannage *breakdown*
    service
department store le grand magasin
depuis *from, since, for*
dernier(-ère) *last* (p 141)
des *of the; some, any* (2.8, 2.7)
descendre★ (descendu) *to go*
    down, get off (bus etc)
    (p 142, 10.4)
désolé(-e) *sorry*
dessus *on it*
deux *two*
deuxième *second*
le diabolo-menthe *lemonade*
    with mint syrup
dimanche m. *(on) Sunday*
dîner *to have dinner*
le dîner-spectacle *dinner with a*
    show
dining room la salle à manger
dinner (to have) dîner
dire *to say*
direct: c'est direct *it's a*
    through train
directement *straight*
la direction *line (métro)*
dish le plat
dix *ten*
dix-huit *eighteen*
dixième *tenth*
dix-neuf *nineteen*
dix-sept *seventeen*
to do faire (p 142)
do you . . . ? (4.4)
doctor le médecin
dog le chien
le domicile *home address*
dommage! *pity!*
donner *to give*
don't ne (n') . . . pas (7.1)
I don't know je ne sais pas
door la porte
double room la chambre
    pour deux personnes
la douche *shower*
doux(-ce) *mild*
douze *twelve*
Dover Douvres

driver le chauffeur
droit: tout droit *straight on*
à droite *to/on the right*
du *of the, from the; some,*
    any (2.8, 2.7)
dur(-e) *hard*

to eat manger
l'eau f. *water*
écossais(-e) *Scottish*
écouter *to listen (to)*
écrire (écrit) *to write* (p 143)
Edinburgh Edimbourg
également *also*
eggs les oeufs m.pl. (11.2)
l'église f. *church*
eh bien *well!*
elle *she, it* (8.7)
elles *they* (9.1, 9.7)
embrasser *to kiss*
l'emplacement m. *pitch*
en *in, into, to* (7.2, 9.1), *on;*
    made of; of it, of them
enchanté(-e) *pleased to meet you*
encore *still, more*
l'enfant m. *child*
engine le moteur
England l'Angleterre f.
English anglais(-e)
English £ la livre sterling
l'ensemble m. résidentiel
    housing complex
ensuite *then, to follow*
entre *between*
l'entrée f. *entrance, entry;*
    admission charge
les environs m.pl. *surroundings*
l'épicerie f. *grocer's*
les épinards m.pl. *spinach*
l'époque f. *time, era*
l'Espagne f. *Spain*
espagnol(-e) *Spanish*
espérer *to hope* (p 141)
essayer *to try (on)*
est *is; has* (10.4)
est-ce que *(introduces a*
    question, 7.8, p 143)
l'estomac m. *stomach*
et *and*

l'étage m. *floor, storey*
était *was*
les Etats-Unis m.pl. *United States*
été *been*
êtes: vous êtes *you are; you*
have (10.4)
l'étoile f. *star*
être *to be* (p 142)
l'étudiant m. (*man*) *student*
l'étudiante f. (*woman*) *student*
evening le soir, la soirée
excursion l'excursion f.
to go on an excursion faire
une excursion
excuse me pardon
je m' excuse *I'm sorry*
exhibition l'exposition f.
expensive cher(-ère) (p 141)
l'exposition f. *exhibition*
extension le poste
extra *the very best*

F, fr. = franc(s)
la fabrication *manufacture*
en face de *opposite*
faire (fait) *to do, make* (p 142);
to go (*Sidelines* p 70)
ça fait *it costs*
ça fait plaisir *it gives pleasure*
faites: vous faites *you do, make*
faites le plein *fill up* (*tank*)
far (*to*) loin
fast vite
father le père
il faut *you have to*
il vous faut *you need*
faux(-sse) *wrong*
feet les pieds m.pl.
la femme *woman, wife*
fermé(-e) *closed*
fermer *to close*
festival le festival
la fête *public holiday*
les feux (rouges) m.pl. *traffic
lights*
la fièvre *temperature*
to fill up faire le plein
la fille *daughter*
la jeune fille *young girl*

la fillette *little girl*
film le film
le fils *son*
to find trouver
finir (fini) *to finish* (p 142)
flat l'appartement m.
flat (*battery, tyre*) à plat
la fleur *flower*
floor l'étage m.
le foie *liver*
font (*they*) *make, do* (9.3)
for pour
forgotten oublié
formidable *great, fantastic*
fortnight quinze jours
four-star petrol le super
les fraises f.pl. *strawberries*
free libre
le frein *brake*
le frère *brother*
Friday vendredi m.
friend l'ami m., l'amie f.
les frites f.pl. *chips, French fries*
froid: il fait froid *it's cold*
from de
le fromage *cheese*
full board la pension
complète
fumer *to smoke*

Galles: le pays de Galles *Wales*
gallois(-e) *Welsh*
garage le garage
le garçon *waiter; boy*
garden le jardin
la gare *station*
la gare routière *bus/coach
station*
se garer *to park*
à gauche *to/on the left*
la gendarmerie *out-of-town police*
generous généreux(-se)
gentil(-le) *kind, nice*
gentlemen messieurs
to get off (*train etc*) descendre★
(p 142, 10.4)
le gigot d'agneau *leg of lamb*
girlfriend l'amie f.
la glace *ice cream*

glass le verre
glasses les lunettes f.pl.
to go aller★ (p 142, 10.3);
faire (*Sidelines* p 70)
to go out sortir★ (p 142, 10.4)
gold en or
golf clubs les clubs m.pl. de
golf
good bon(-ne)
goodbye au revoir
good evening bonsoir
good-looking beau (f. belle)
(8.5)
good morning bonjour
goodnight bonne nuit
grand(-e) *big, large, tall*
la Grande Bretagne *Great Britain*
grape le raisin
gratuit(-e) *free* (*of charge*)
great formidable
green vert(-e)
grey gris(-e)
la grotte *cave*
le guichet *ticket office*
guide le guide
guide book le guide
guided tour la visite guidée

h = heure(s)
habiter *to live* (*in a place*)
hairdresser le coiffeur (*man*),
la coiffeuse (*woman*)
half (*a*) demi- . . .
half past et demie
ham le jambon
handbag le sac (à main)
hard dur(-e)
has a; est (10.4)
hat le chapeau
to have avoir (p 142)
you have to il faut
he il
headache mal m. à la tête
headlights les phares m.pl.
hello bonjour; allô (*on phone*)
to help aider
her son, sa, ses (8.6)
here ici
l'heure f. *time, hour, o'clock*

hier *yesterday*
to hire louer
his son, sa, ses (8.6)
holiday les vacances f.pl.
at home à la maison
l'homme m. *man*
l'horaire m. *timetable*
hot chaud(-e)
hotel l'hôtel m.
l'hôtel m. de ville *town hall*
hour l'heure f.
house la maison
housewife la ménagère
how do I/we get to pour
    aller à
how much combien
how old is . . . quel âge a . . .?
l'huile f. *oil*
huit *eight*
les huîtres f.pl. *oysters*
husband le mari
hypermarket l'hypermarché m.

I je (j'); moi *(emphatic)*
    (6.1, 6.3)
ice cream la glace
ici *here*
il *he, it* (8.7)
il y a *there is, there are*
ill malade
ils *they* (9.7)
important buildings les
    monuments m.pl.
in à, en, dans
l'indicatif m. *dialling code*
indiqué(-e) *signposted*
inoubliable *unforgettable*
intelligent intelligent(-e)
interdit(-e) *prohibited*
interesting intéressant(-e)
to introduce présenter
Irish irlandais(-e)
is est
it is c'est
it il, elle (8.7); ce (c')
Italian italien(-ne)
Italy l'Italie f.

j' = je

jaloux(-se) *jealous*
le jardin *garden*
je *I*
jeudi m. *(on) Thursday*
jeune *young*
joli(-e) *pretty*
jouer *to play*
le jour *day*
le journal (pl. journaux)
    newspaper
journalist le journaliste
la journée *day*
jusqu'à *as far as, until*

key la clé
kind gentil(-le)
I know (a fact) je sais
to know (people, places)
    connaître (p 142)

l' = le, la
la *the* (2.5)
là *there, in*
là-bas *over there, down there*
la laine *wool*
laisser *to leave (behind)*
le lait *milk*
lamp la lampe
language la langue
large grand(-e)
last dernier(-ère) (p 141)
le *the* (2.5); *it; him*
leather en cuir
to leave partir* (p 142, 10.4)
la leçon *lesson*
le légume *vegetable*
lemonade la limonade
les *the* (2.5); *them*
letter la lettre
letterbox la boîte aux lettres
leur(s) *their* (9.6)
libre *free, unoccupied, spaces*
    available
le lieu *place*
lift l'ascenseur m.
light: have you a light? vous
    avez du feu?
lighter le briquet
la ligne *number (bus), line (métro)*

like: I'd like je voudrais;
    we'd like nous voulons
to like aimer
to listen (to) écouter
le lit *bed*
    à deux lits *twin-bedded*
    le grand lit *double bed*
litre le litre
little petit(-e)
a little un peu (de)
to live (in) habiter
la livre *pound*
la location *hire*
loin *far (to), a long way*
le loisir *leisure*
Londres *London*
longtemps *long, a long time*
to look at regarder
lost perdu
a lot beaucoup
louer *to hire, rent*
to love aimer
lovely agréable
lunch le déjeuner
lundi m. *(on) Monday*

m = mètre(s)
m' = me *me*
ma *my* (6.2)
le magasin *shop*
    le grand magasin
    department store
la mairie *town hall*
mais *but*
la maison *house*
to make faire (p 142)
mal *bad*
le mal à la tête *headache*
le mal à l'estomac *stomach ache*
malade *ill*
man l'homme m.
manager le patron
manageress la patronne
manger *to eat*
le marché *market*
marcher *to work, function*
mardi m. *(on) Tuesday*
le mari *husband*
marié(-e) *married*

market le marché
le Maroc *Morocco*
married marié(-e)
marron *brown (never changes)*
match le match
le matin *(in the) morning*
may I/one je peux, on peut? (7.7, 7.9)
me me (m')
meat la viande
le médicament *medicine*
même *same*
to mend réparer
menu la carte
le menu *set meal*
la mer *sea*
merci *thank you; no thanks*
merci beaucoup/bien *thank you very much*
mercredi m. *(on) Wednesday*
la mère *mother*
mes *my* (6.2)
message le message
la messe *mass*
messieurs *gentlemen*
messieurs-dames *(polite way to address mixed company)*
les meubles m.pl. *furniture*
(at) midday (à) midi
midi *noon, twelve pm*
le Midi *South of France*
midnight minuit
milk le lait
mille, mil *thousand*
(à) minuit *(at) midnight*
moi *I, me* (6.1, 6.3)
moins *less*
moins cher *something cheaper*
le mois *month*
mon *my* (6.2)
Monday lundi m.
mondial: le centre mondial *world centre*
money l'argent m.
la monnaie *(small) change*
monsieur *Mr, sir, dear Sir; man; waiter!*
monsieur l'agent *officer!*

monter* *to go up, to get on (bus etc); to take up*
le monument *important building, monument*
le morceau *piece*
morning le matin
le moteur *engine*
mother la mère
motorway l'autoroute f.
museum le musée
my mon, ma, mes (6.2)

n' = ne
nager *to swim*
la naissance *birth*
ne (n') . . . pas *not, don't* (7.1)
n'est-ce pas *isn't it, don't you? etc (Sidelines p 71)*
neuf *nine*
newspaper le journal (pl. journaux)
next prochain(-e)
nice gentil(-le)
no non, pas de
noir(-e) *black*
le nom *name*
nombreux(-se) *numerous, great many*
non *no, not*
non pas *not*
Normandy la Normandie
nos *our* (6.4)
not ne (n') . . . pas (6.1, 7.1)
la note *(hotel) bill*
notre *our* (6.4)
nous *we, us*
la nuit *night*
number (bus) la ligne
le numéro *number*
faire le numéro *to dial*

s'occuper de *to look after*
o'clock heure(s) (4.8)
l'oeuf m. *egg* (11.2)
of de (d')
office le bureau
officer! monsieur l'agent
offrir *to offer, give (a present)*
oil l'huile f.

OK d'accord
old vieux, vieil (f. vieille) (8.5)
omelette l'omelette f.
on *one, we, you, people, they* (7.9)
on à, en, sur
one on (7.9); un, une (2.3)
ont *(they) have* (9.3)
onze *eleven*
open ouvert(-e)
to open ouvrir (p 142)
opera (house) l'opéra m.
or ou
l'or m. *gold*
orange l'orange f.
l'ordinaire m. *two-star petrol*
ou *or*
ou bien *or else*
où *where*
oublier *to forget*
oui *yes*
our notre, nos (6.4)
ouvert(-e) *open*
ouvrir *to open* (p 142)

packet le paquet
le pain *bread*
le palais de justice *law courts*
en panne *broken down*
le pantalon *trousers*
le paquet *packet*
par *by, through, per*
par ici *round here, this way, around*
parents les parents m.pl.
le parfum *perfume*
la parfumerie *perfumery, perfume factory*
to park se garer
le parking *car park*
parler *to speak*
la part: c'est de la part de qui? *who's calling?*
partir* (parti) *to leave* (p 142, 10.4)
à partir de *as from*
pas *not*
pas de *no*

passer *to spend*; *to go*
passport le passeport
la pâtisserie *pastry, cake*;
    pastry/cake shop
le patron *manager, owner, boss*
la patronne *manageress,*
    manager's wife
payant *fee payable*
le pays *country*
à péage *toll payable*
la pêche *peach*; *fishing*
la peinture *painting*
perdu *lost* (10.1)
le père *father*
perfume le parfum
petit(-e) *small, little*
petrol station la station-
    service
un peu (de) *a little*
on peut? *can one/may I?* (7.9)
peut-être *perhaps*
ils peuvent *they can*
je peux? *can/may I?* (7.7)
les phares m.pl. *headlights*
photo la photo
piece le morceau
la pièce *coin*
la pièce d'identité *means of*
    identification
à pied *on foot*
pipi wee wee
la piscine *swimming pool*
pity: that's a pity c'est
    dommage
la place *square*; *seat*
la plage *beach*
au plaisir de *looking forward to*
le plaisir *pleasure*
plan le projet
le plan (de la ville) *(town) map*
la planche à voile: faire de la
    planche à voile *to go*
    windsurfing
le plat *dish*
to play (football, tennis etc)
    jouer (au football etc)
please s'il vous/te plaît
pleased content(-e)
le plein! *fill up (tank)*

plus *more*
le plus *most*
le pneu *tyre*
à point *medium done (meat)*
pois: les petits pois *peas*
le poisson *fish*
le pompiste *forecourt attendant*
le pont *bridge*
la porte *door, gate*
postcard la carte postale
la poste *post office*
le poste *extension*
le poulet *chicken*
pound la livre
la poupée *doll*
pour *for, to, in order to*
pour aller à *how do I/we get to*
pour cent *per cent*
pouvoir *to be able (to)* (p 142)
pratiquer *to practise*
to prefer préférer (p 141)
préféré(-e) *favourite*
premier(-ère) *first* (p 141)
prendre (pris) *to take*; *to*
    catch (train etc) (p 142)
ils prennent *they take*
le prénom *first name, forename*
près de *near*
présenter *to introduce*
la pression *pressure (tyre)*
pretty joli(-e)
pris *taken* (10.1)
private privé(-e)
le prix *price, fee, charge*
    dans tous les prix *at all*
    different prices
problem le problème
prochain(-e) *next*
le projet *plan*
la promenade *walk, trip*
    la promenade
    équestre *ride*
    faire une promenade *to go*
    for a walk
à propos *by the way*
puis *then*
le pull *jumper*

qu' = que

le quai *platform*
quand *when*
quarante *forty*
le quartier *part of town, area*
quatre *four*
quatre-vingts *eighty*
quatrième *fourth*
que (qu') *as, that*
quel(-le) *which, what* (p 140)
quelque chose (de) *something*
qu'est-ce que *what*
qui *who, which*
quiet tranquille
quinze *fifteen*
quinze jours *fortnight*
ne quittez pas *hold the line*

racket la raquette
to rain pleuvoir
le raisin *grape*
rappeler *to call back* (p 141)
rate le tarif
rate (of exchange) le cours
to recommend conseiller
record le disque
red rouge
regarder *to watch, look round*
régler *to settle (bill)*
je regrette *I'm sorry*
(se) rencontrer *to meet (each other)*
les renseignements m.pl.
    information
réparer *to mend, repair*
répond: ça ne répond pas
    no answer
restaurant le restaurant
restaurant car le wagon-
    restaurant
il reste *there is . . . left*
rester* *to stay, remain* (10.4)
retired retraité(-e)
le retour *return*
revenir* (revenu) *to go*
    back, return (p 142)
rich riche
rien *nothing*
de rien *you're welcome (in*
    answer to thanks)
le riz *rice*

roadside restaurant le relais routier
room la chambre
rose la rose
rôti roast
rouge red
round here par ici
la route *road, highway*
  bonne route! *safe journey!*
la route nationale *'A' road*
rowboat le canot
rowing: to go rowing faire du canotage
la rue *street*

s' = se; = si
sa *his, her, its* (8.6)
le sac (à main) *handbag*
le sachet de thé *teabag*
saignant *rare, underdone (meat)*
sailboard la planche à voile
sailing: to go sailing faire de la voile
je sais *I know (a fact)*
la salle *hall, auditorium, room*
la salle à manger *dining room*
salut! *hi!*
samedi m. *(on) Saturday*
sandwich le sandwich
sans *without*
Saturday samedi m.
sauf (sf.) *except*
le savon *soap*
le scotch *sellotape*
Scottish écossais(-e)
se (s') *oneself, each other*
seat la place
to see voir
  see you à tout à l'heure
  see you tomorrow à demain
  self-drive sans chauffeur
la semaine *week*
sensationnel(-le) *terrific*
sept *seven*
seront (they) *will be*
ses *his, her, its* (8.6)
set meal le menu
le shampooing *shampoo*
she elle

shirt la chemise
shop le magasin
shopping: to do the shopping faire les courses
show le spectacle
shower la douche
si (s') *if; so*
sick: to feel sick avoir mal au coeur
le siècle *century*
signposted indiqué(-e)
silver en argent
single (ticket) l'aller m. simple
sister la soeur
le ski: faire du ski (nautique) *to go (water) skiing*
small petit(-e)
to smoke fumer
so si
la société *company*
le soir *(in the) evening*
la soirée *evening, evening entertainment*
soixante *sixty*
soixante-dix *seventy*
soixante-dix-huitième *seventy-eighth*
soixante et onze *seventy-one*
en solde *in the sale*
le soleil *sun*
some du, de la, de l', des (2.8)
sommes: nous sommes *we are; we have* (10.4)
son *his, her, its* (8.6)
son le fils
ils sont *they are; they have* (10.4)
sore feet mal m. aux pieds
sore throat mal m. à la gorge
I'm sorry je regrette
la sortie *exit, way out*
sortir* (sorti) *to go/come out* (p 142, 10.4)
soup la soupe
souple *soft*
sous le règne *in the reign*
souvenir le souvenir
souvent *often*
Spanish espagnol(-e)
to speak parler

speaking: who's speaking? qui est à l'appareil?
special spécial(-e)
le spectacle *show*
to spend passer
spinach les épinards m.pl.
stamp le timbre
to start commencer
station la gare
la station *resort*
le stationnement *parking*
stationner *to park*
to stay rester* (10.4)
student (woman) l'étudiante f.
je suis *I am; I have* (10.4)
suitcase la valise
Sunday dimanche m.
suntan oil l'huile f. pour bronzer
le super *four-star petrol*
supermarket le supermarché
suppository le suppositoire
sur *on, of, over, about*
sûr(-e) *certain*
svp = s'il vous plaît
swimming pool la piscine
swim-suit le maillot de bain
sympa *nice (colloquial)*
sympathique *nice, friendly*
le syndicat d'initiative *tourist office*

le tabac *tobacconist's-cum-newsagent's*
le tableau *picture, painting*
tablet le comprimé
la taille *size (clothes)*
to take prendre (p 142)
  take a seat prenez place
la tapisserie *tapestry*
la tasse *cup*
taxi le taxi
te *you (familiar)* (16.5)
tea le thé
telephone le téléphone
television la télé
temperature la fièvre
tennis court le court de tennis
le terrain de golf *golf course*
terrific sensationnel(-le)

la tête *head*

le TGV (= train à grande vitesse) *high speed train*

thank you merci

that is c'est

the le, l', la, les (2.5)

le thé *tea*

theatre le théâtre

their leur(s) (9.6)

there is/are il y a

they ils, elles (9.7)

third troisième

this ce, cet, cette (10.2)

Thursday jeudi m.

ticket le billet, le ticket

le timbre *stamp*

time: at what time à quelle heure

tin opener l'ouvre-boîtes f.

le tire-bouchon *corkscrew*

to à, en (7.2, 9.1), pour, jusqu'à

today aujourd'hui

toi *you (familiar, emphatic)*

toilets les toilettes f.pl.

tomorrow demain

ton *your (familiar)* (16.5)

toothache mal m. aux dents

toothbrush la brosse à dents

toujours *always*

la tour *tower*

tourner *to turn*

tous m.pl. *all, every*

tous les deux *both*

tous les jours/soirs *every day/evening*

tout(-e) *all, every*

à tout à l'heure *see you*

tout confort *all mod cons*

tout de suite *immediately*

de tout *some of everything*

toute (la nuit) *all (night)*

toutes les . . . *every . . .*

towel la serviette

town la ville

town hall l'hôtel m. de ville, la mairie

town map le plan de la ville

train le train

la tranche *slice*

le travail *work*

travailler *to work*

le traveller *traveller's cheque*

traveller's cheque le chèque de voyage, le traveller

traverser *to cross*

treize *thirteen*

trente *thirty*

très *very*

trois *three*

trop *too much*

le trottoir *pavement*

trousers le pantalon

se trouver *to be (situated)*

tu *you (familiar)* (p 142)

Tuesday mardi m.

typical typique

tyre le pneu

un/une *a(n); one* (2.1, 2.2)

to understand comprendre (p 142)

unemployed au chômage

until jusqu'à

va *goes/is going (to)* (8.2); (see also 8.8)

ça va *OK, how are things/you?*

on va? *shall we?* (7.9)

les vacances f.pl. *holidays*

je vais *I'm going (to)* (7.2, 7.3)

la valise *suitcase*

le veau *veal*

le vélo *bike*

faire du vélo *to go cycling*

la vendeuse *(woman) shop assistant*

vendredi m. *(on) Friday*

venir* (venu) *to come* (p 142, 10.4)

vérifier *to check*

le verre *glass*

vers *about*

very très

veulent *(they) want (to)*

veut *(he/she) wants (to)*

veux *(I/you) want (to)*

la viande *meat*

vieil (f. vieille) *old* (8.5)

ils viennent *they come*

vieux (f. vieille) *old* (8.5)

la ville *town*

le vin *wine*

vinegar le vinaigre

vingt *twenty*

to visit visiter

vite *fast*

les vitraux m.pl. *stained-glass windows*

voici *here is/are*

voilà *there is/are; there you are*

la voile: faire de la voile *to go sailing*

voir (vu) *to see* (10.1)

en voiture *by car*

la voiture *car*

la voiture de location *hire car*

ils vont *they go; they are (well etc)* (9.2)

vos *your* (9.5)

votre *your* (9.5)

je voudrais *I'd like (to)*

vouloir *to want/like (to)* (p 142)

vous *you, to you, yourself*

le voyage *journey, trip*

le voyage de noces *honeymoon*

le voyageur *traveller*

vu *seen* (10.1)

la vue *view*

le wagon-restaurant *restaurant car*

to wait (for) attendre (p 142)

waiter! monsieur, garçon

waitress! mademoiselle

Wales le pays de Galles

to want (to) vouloir (p 142)

it was c'était

to watch regarder

water skiing: to go water skiing faire du ski nautique

we nous

Wednesday mercredi m.

week la semaine

Welsh gallois(-e)

went (*see* aller, 10.3; faire
    10.1, *Sidelines* p 70)
what qu'est-ce que; quel(-le)
what is . . . like? comment
    est . . . ?
what sort of qu'est-ce
    que . . . comme
when quand
where où
which quel(-le) (p 140)
white blanc (f. blanche)
who qui

wife la femme
windscreen le pare-brise
windsurfing: to go windsurfing
    faire de la planche à voile
wine le vin
wine cellar la cave
with avec
without sans
woman la femme
work le travail
to work travailler; marcher
    (*function*)

to write écrire (p 143)

y in it; there
le yaourt *yogurt*
year l'an m., l'année f.
yes oui
yesterday hier
you vous
young jeune
your votre, vos (9.5)

zut! *damn*

MENU TERMS

Food

agneau *lamb*
ail *garlic*
aïoli *mayonnaise with garlic*
amandes *almonds*
ananas *pineapple*
anchois *anchovies*
andouillette *small sausage made
    of chitterlings*
(à l')anglaise *boiled, steamed*
anguille *eel*
artichauts *artichokes*
asperges *asparagus*
assiette anglaise *assorted cold
    meats*
(à la) basquaise *with ham,
    peppers, tomatoes, garlic, onions*
beignet *fritter*
bifteck *steak*
bisque *chowder*
blanquette de veau *veal in white
    sauce*
boeuf *beef*
bouchée à la reine *chicken vol-
    au-vent*
bouillabaisse *fish soup speciality
    from Provence*
brandade *prepared cod with cream
    and garlic*
(à la) broche *cooked on a spit*
(en) brochette *on a skewer*
cabillaud *cod*
canard *duck*

carbon(n)ade *charcoal-grilled meat*
cassoulet *meat and bean stew*
cèpes *(wild) mushrooms*
cerises *cherries*
cervelles *brains*
charcuterie *pork meats*
chasseur *with mushrooms,
    tomatoes, herbs etc*
châteaubriand *thick steak*
chicorée *endive*
chips *crisps*
chou *cabbage*
choucroute *sauerkraut*
chou-fleur *cauliflower*
colin *hake*
compote *stewed fruit*
concombre *cucumber*
confiture *jam*
contre-filet *kind of T-bone steak*
coquilles St-Jacques *scallops*
cornichons *gherkins*
côtelette *chop*
crème Chantilly/fouettée *whipped
    cream*
crêpe *pancake*
crevettes *shrimps, prawns*
croque-monsieur, croque-
    madame *toasted sandwich
    with cheese, ham etc*
(en) croûte *in pastry*
cru *raw*
crudités *raw vegetables*
crustacés *shellfish*

cuisses de grenouille *frogs' legs*
daurade *sea bream*
dinde *turkey*
écrevisses *(freshwater) crayfish*
endive *chicory*
entrecôte *rib steak*
entrée *first course*
épaule *shoulder*
épinards *spinach*
escargots *snails*
farci *stuffed*
faux-filet *kind of T-bone steak*
fenouil *fennel*
(au) feu de bois *charcoal-grilled*
fines herbes *(fresh) herbs*
flageolets *dwarf kidney beans*
flan *custard tart*
foie *liver*
forestière *with bacon, potatoes,
    mushrooms*
(au) four *baked*
frais (fraîche) *fresh, chilled*
fraises *strawberries*
framboises *raspberries*
frappé *iced, chilled*
frit *fried*
frites *chips, French fries*
friture *mixed fried fish*
fruits de mer *seafood*
fumé *smoked*
garni *served with vegetables,
    salads etc*
(en) gelée *in aspic, jellied*

gigot *leg (of lamb)*
glacé *iced, glazed*
grillade *grilled meat*
haché *minced*
hareng *herring*
haricots verts *green beans*
homard *lobster*
huîtres *oysters*
jambon *ham*
langouste *kind of lobster*
langoustines *large prawns*
langue *tongue*
lapin *rabbit*
légumes *vegetables*
loup de mer *sea bass*
maison *chef's speciality*
maquereau *mackerel*
marrons *chestnuts*
merlan *whiting*
merlu, merluche *hake*
meunière *cooked in butter*
miel *honey*
mignon *tenderloin*
moules (marinière) *mussels (in white wine)*
mousseline *light creamy sauce*
nature *plain*
navarin *mutton stew*
noisettes *hazelnuts*
noix *choice cut of meat; walnuts*
oeuf à la coque *boiled egg*
oeuf brouillé *scrambled egg*
oeuf dur *hard-boiled egg*
oeuf poché *poached egg*
oeuf sur le plat *fried egg*
oignons *onions*
pamplemousse *grapefruit*
panné *in breadcrumbs*
parmentier *made with potatoes*
pastèque *watermelon*
pâtes fraîches *fresh pasta*
(du) pays *locally grown or produced*
(au) persil, persillé *with parsley*
piperade *Basque dish with peppers, tomatoes, eggs*

plateau de fromage *cheese board*
poire (Belle Hélène) *pear (with ice cream and chocolate sauce)*
poireaux *leeks*
poivrons *green peppers*
pommes *apples*
pommes (de terre) *potatoes*
pommes allumettes *matchstick potatoes*
pommes vapeur *steamed potatoes*
potage *soup*
pot-au-feu *pot-roast (beef) with vegetables*
poularde *capon*
poulet *chicken*
poussin *baby chicken*
primeurs *early vegetables*
(à la) provençale *cooked with herbs, tomatoes, onions, olives, garlic*
quenelles *light sausage-shaped dumplings made with minced fish or meat*
radis *radishes*
ragoût *stew*
râpé *grated*
rillettes *potted meat, usually pork*
ris de veau *sweetbreads*
riz *rice*
rognons *kidneys*
rosbif *roast beef*
rôti *roast*
rouget *red mullet*
salade niçoise *salad with tunny, eggs, tomatoes, olives, anchovies etc*
saucisse *sausage (for frying)*
saucisson *sausage (for slicing)*
saumon *salmon*
selle *saddle*
steak tartare *raw minced beef*
(au) sucre *(with) sugar*
sur commande *special order*
(en) sus *not included*
terrine *special meat or fish pâté*
thon *tunny*

tournedos *thick fillet steak*
truffé *with truffles*
truite *trout*
vacherin *meringue-type dessert*
vapeur *steamed*
veau *veal*
velouté *creamy soup*
viande *meat*
volaille *poultry*
yaourt *yogurt*

Drink

bière blonde *lager*
bière brune *ale*
bière pression *draught beer*
boissons *drinks*
café crème *white coffee (with milk, not cream)*
café (au) lait *coffee with milk*
café nature/noir/express *black coffee*
cassis *blackcurrant liqueur*
citron pressé *freshly squeezed lemon juice*
diabolo-menthe *lemonade with mint syrup*
doux *sweet (for wine, cider)*
glaçons *ice cubes*
grand cru *wine of exceptional quality*
infusion *herbal tea*
jus de fruit *fruit juice*
kir *white wine with blackcurrant liqueur*
lait *milk*
mousseux *sparkling*
panaché *shandy*
pastis *aniseed-flavoured aperitif*
pichet *jug of wine*
sec *dry*
thé citron *tea with lemon*
thé (au) lait *tea with milk*
thé nature *black tea*
vin d'appellation *quality wine*